Workbook and Anthology

for use with

Harmony in Context

Second Edition

Miguel A. Roig-Francolí
University of Cincinnati

Luke
+
Colton
4ever

Published by McGraw-Hill, an imprint of The McGraw-Hill Companies, Inc., 1221 Avenue of the Americas, New York, NY 10020. Copyright © 2011, 2003. All rights reserved. No part of this publication may be reproduced or distributed in any form or by any means, or stored in a database or retrieval system, without the prior written consent of The McGraw-Hill Companies, Inc., including, but not limited to, in any network or other electronic storage or transmission, or broadcast for distance learning.

This book is printed on acid-free paper.

2 3 4 5 6 7 8 9 0 QDB/QDB 1

ISBN: 978-0-07-313795-7
MHID: 0-07-313795-2

Cover: Vicente Pascual. *Aquatio I,* mixed media on canvas. 2005. © Artists Rights Society, New York/VEGAP, Madrid.

The Internet addresses listed in the text were accurate at the time of publication. The inclusion of a Web site does not indicate an endorsement by the authors or McGraw-Hill, and McGraw-Hill does not guarantee the accuracy of the information presented at these sites.

www.mhhe.com

Preface

This workbook is meant to be used in conjunction with the study of the textbook *Harmony in Context*. The textbook provides, at the end of each chapter, a set of exercises in the form of a worksheet. A second set of exercises for each chapter is provided in this workbook. Exercises here are similar to, but not always of the exact same type as, those found in the corresponding worksheet. Both sets for each chapter begin with several analytical exercises, followed by writing and composition exercises of many types: chord spelling and recognition, realization of short and long progressions based on given Roman numerals, realization of figured basses, harmonization of melodies, composition of keyboard-style accompaniments, composition of original harmonic progressions, and so on. Instructors may want to use one of the two sets for practice in class and the other one for homework assignments, or they may choose to use one of the sets as a pool of possible questions to be used in quizzes and exams.

Chapters also include an assignment of keyboard harmony in which the chords and most standard progressions studied in each chapter are practiced at the piano in a variety of keys and through a variety of exercises. Playing and practicing these keyboard exercises will reinforce the understanding of the harmonic materials studied in the book, and will help students familiarize themselves with the sound of specific harmonic progressions.

Finally, this volume also includes an anthology of fifty-nine musical excerpts and complete pieces by twenty-six composers ranging from the sixteenth century to the twentieth century. The anthology is widely used as a source of examples from the literature throughout both the textbook and the workbook, and it allows for analyses of and references to numerous complete pieces or movements which otherwise could not have been addressed. Because of this close relationship between the book and the anthology, the latter is not meant to be an optional supplement to the book, but rather an essential and required component of the pedagogical packet.

Contents

INTRODUCTION

The Fundamentals
of Music

g.   Wagner

TONIC   TONIC TRIAD   RANGE   MODE/KEY   SCALE:

Lydian

h.

Scotland

TONIC   TONIC TRIAD   RANGE   MODE/KEY   SCALE:

Phrygian

KEYBOARD EXERCISES   Play the following exercises at the keyboard with the right hand. Examples for each of the exercises are provided in example D.2.

1. Be able to play M, m, ° and ⁺ triads in root position on any note.

2. Be able to play the diatonic triads on each of the scale degrees in the following keys:

    CM, GM, FM, DM, and B♭M

    Am, Em, Dm, Bm, and Gm

    In minor keys, use the harmonic minor scale (except for the triad on $\hat{3}$, which you should play as a M triad).

3. Play the following triads in first inversions:

    CM, GM, FM, DM, B♭M, AM, E♭M, EM, A♭M, BM, D♭M, F♯M

    Am, Em, Dm, Bm, Gm, F♯m, Cm, C♯m, Fm, G♯m, B♭m, D♯m

4. Play the same triads in second inversion.

 Example D.2

1.

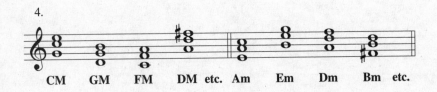

2.

3.

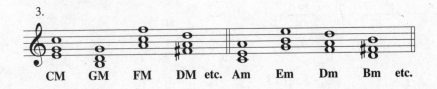

4.

EXERCISE 9   Analysis.

Texture. On a separate sheet, briefly discuss the texture of the following examples:

a) Anthology, no. 32, Beethoven, Piano Sonata in Fm, op. 2, no. 1, mm. 1–8.

b) Anthology, no. 22, Chevalier de Saint–Georges, Violin Concerto.

c) Anthology, no. 27, Mozart, Piano Sonata in AM, mm. 1–8.

d) Anthology, no. 26, Mozart, Piano Sonata in CM, III.

e) Example E.3.

f) Anthology, no. 15, J. S. Bach, *The Well-Tempered Clavier*, I, Fugue no. 11 in FM

In each of these examples, answer the following questions:

1) Is it homophonic or polyphonic (contrapuntal)?

2) If it is homophonic, what kind of accompaniment does it feature?
   a. Melody with block chords.
   b. Melody with broken (arpeggiated) chords.
   c. Melody, chords, and a parallel supporting melody.
   d. Accompaniment (mostly) homorhythmic with melody.
   e. Other (explain).

3) If it is polyphonic, explain the exact relationship among voices.
   a. Chorale texture.
   b. Free counterpoint: voices unrelated, nonimitative counterpoint.
   c. Imitative counterpoint: voices share same thematic material.
   d. All voices are similar in importance.

♪♪♪ Example E.3   Antonio de Cabezón, *Diferencias sobre el Canto del Caballero*

KEYBOARD EXERCISES   Play the following exercises at the keyboard with the right hand. Examples for each of the exercises are provided in example E.4.

1. Play the triads represented by the following Roman numerals in each of the following M keys:

    I, V, ii, vii°, IV, vi, iii

    CM, GM, FM, DM, AND B♭M

    Play the triads represented by the following Roman numerals in each of the following m keys:

    i, iv, VI, V, vii°, III, ii°

    Am, Em, Dm, Bm, and Gm

2. Play the following chords in each of the keys from exercise 1:

    M: I_6, V_6, ii_6, $vii°_6$, IV_6, vi_6, iii_6

    m: i_6, iv_6, VI_6, $vii°_6$, III_6, $ii°_6$

3. Play the following chords in each of the keys from keyboard exercise 1:

    M: I_4^6, IV_4^6, V_4^6

    m: i_4^6, iv_4^6, V_4^6

Example E.4

1.

CM: I   V   ii   vii°   etc.   Am: i   iv   VI   V   etc.

2.

CM: I_6 V_6 ii_6 etc.   Am: i_6 iv_6 VI_6 etc.

3.

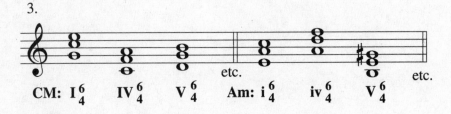

CM: I_4^6 IV_4^6 V_4^6 Am: i_4^6 iv_4^6 V_4^6 etc.

PART 1

Diatonic Harmony

Chapter 2

The Tonic and Dominant Triads
in Root Position

EXERCISE 1   Analysis. Study example 2.1.

1. What is the key of the piece? (Careful: note that this little dance piece does not begin on the tonic.)

2. Analyze the complete example with Roman numerals (RN). Notice that the left hand uses the *bass afterbeat* keyboard pattern, and that *the complete measure* is analyzed as one chord, with the position determined by the bass on the downbeat.

   a) On what harmony does this piece begin?

   b) On what two chords is the piece based?

   c) The first section of the piece (mm. 1–8) has two phrases (1–4 and 5–8). Is there any difference between the two phrases? What kind of cadence occurs in mm. 4 and 8?

   d) The second section (mm. 9–16) also contains two phrases (9–12 and 13–16). How are they related? Are the cadences in mm. 12 and 16 the same? Identify the cadence type for both of them.

   e) Is the complete melody based on a short rhythmic pattern (a rhythmic motive)? Write this rhythmic pattern here:

Example 2.1   Franz Schubert, Originaltänze, op. 9, no. 25

f) Compare the melody in mm. 1–8 and 9–16. The basic principle by which these two melodies are related is called *inversion*. Examine carefully the melodies (focus, for instance, on mm. 1 and 9) and explain precisely what *inversion* is.

3. Provide a brief explanation of the formal role of the I–V–I progression in the following two fragments: anthology, no. 28 (Mozart, Piano Sonata in B♭M, K. 333, III, mm. 1–8), and anthology, no. 26 (Mozart, Piano Sonata in CM, K. 309, III, mm. 1–19). Play or listen to these examples. Determine their phrase and cadential structure, and discuss the role of I and V in shaping the form of these fragments.

KEYBOARD HARMONY

1. Play the following keyboard progressions and listen to the chords and their connections as you play. Play them in several keys. Begin with CM and Cm, and then play them in major and minor modes on G, D, and F (except for example 2.2a, which you should be able to play in all M and m keys).

Example 2.2

Notice that these progressions are written in *keyboard texture,* rather than four-part vocal texture. In chordal keyboard texture, it is customary to play the bass alone with the left hand, and the three remaining voices in close position with the right hand. All the same voice-leading rules studied in this and the previous chapters apply to keyboard block-chord style.

2. Refer to example 2.3 in the textbook. Play the soprano-bass patterns in that example at the piano, adding inner voices in keyboard texture, in major and minor modes on C, G, D, and F.

Chapter 3

Harmonic Function; The Subdominant Triad in Root Position

EXERCISE 1 Analysis.

1. Example 3.1.
   a) Analyze the passage with RNs (Roman numerals).
   b) What is the function of the chord in m. 100? Explain its voice leading and how it relates to the previous and following chord.

   c) Study the voice leading for the whole passage, focusing especially on the right hand. Does it conform with the voice-leading guidelines we studied in chapters 2 and 3?

2. Example 3.2. Study the progression in this excerpt. Analyze it with RNs. Compare its voice leading with the voice leading for this progression studied in this chapter and comment on your comparison.

3. Anthology, no. 56 (Clara Schumann, Trio). On what type of cadence does Clara Schumann end this piece? Can you identify any specific voice-leading licenses taken in the left hand of the piano (mm. 284–285)? This type of open voicing is characteristic for the lower register of the piano, and open fifths provide a very strong harmonic support for such broad instrumental sonorities. The deliberate parallel voicing used here by C. Schumann may be found in instrumental writing and should not be considered a voice-leading "mistake."

Example 3.1   W. A. Mozart, Piano Sonata in AM, K. 331, III, mm. 97–109

Example 3.2   Giuseppe Verdi, *La forza del destino*, act IV, scene 4

Le mi - nac - cie, i fie - ri ac - cen - ti, por - tin se - co in pre - da i ven - ti, per - do -
na - te - mi pie - tà,   O fra - tel, pie - tà, pie - tà.

KEYBOARD HARMONY

1. Play and learn the progressions in example 3.7 of the textbook. Listen to the role of the subdominant in these elaborations of the I–V–I progression.

2. Play the following keyboard progressions in the following major keys: C, F, G, and D; and in the following minor keys: C, A, D, and E.

♪♪ Example 3.3

3. Soprano-bass patterns. Refer to example 3.6 in the textbook. Play the soprano-bass patterns in that example at the piano, adding inner voices in keyboard texture in the same major and minor keys listed previously in keyboard exercise 2.

4. Roman-numeral realization. To practice realization of Roman-numeral progressions, realize the following exercises at the piano, using keyboard texture: textbook, worksheet 3, exercise 2; and workbook, chapter 3, exercise 2.

5. Melody harmonization. To practice melody harmonization, realize the following exercises at the piano, using keyboard texture: textbook, worksheet 3, exercise 3; and workbook, chapter 3, exercise 3.

Chapter 4

Triads in First Inversion

EXERCISE 1   Analysis.

1. The harmonic phrase in example 4.1 is a prolongation of I. Analyze with RNs (Roman numerals). (Notice that the first inversion of V_7 is labeled V_5^6, a chord very similar to V_6), and explain the prolongation of I in terms of voice leading.

| Example 4.1 | Felix Mendelssohn, "Im Grünen," from *Zwölf Gesänge*, op. 8, no. 11, mm. 14–15. |

2. Analyze mm. 15–16 and 18–19 of example 4.2 with RNs. Measure 15, beats 1–2, presents an incomplete chord, which could be read as an A or an F chord if we imply the missing pitch. If we consider the F chord in beats 3–4, and by analogy with m. 16 (all of it is one chord), we will hear the complete m. 15 as an F chord. The symbol V_{4-3}^{6-5}, which will be explained in chapter 7, should be interpreted as a dominant chord (the $\frac{5}{3}$) embellished melodically by the preceding $\frac{6}{4}$ (which we call a "cadential $\frac{6}{4}$").

   a) What is the role of first-inversion chords in this passage? Mark all changes of position with a bracket, and explain them.

   b) What kind of cadence occurs in m. 21?

♪♪ Example 4.2   W. A. Mozart, Piano Sonata in CM, K. 309, I, mm. 15–21

EXERCISE 2   Write the following triads in four voices with correct doubling.

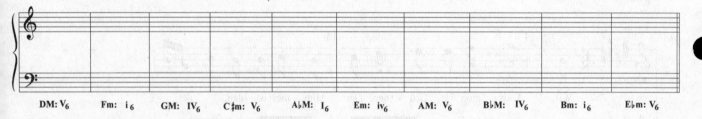

DM: V₆   Fm: i₆   GM: IV₆   C♯m: V₆   A♭M: I₆   Em: iv₆   AM: V₆   B♭M: IV₆   Bm: i₆   E♭m: V₆

EXERCISE 3   Realize the following progressions in four voices. Use voice exchange where possible. *Always verify (and enjoy) the sound of what you write* by playing and listening to it.

Bm: i   i₆   iv   iv₆   V   A♭M: I   IV   V   V₆   I

EXERCISE 4   *Figured bass realization.* Provide a RN analysis and a four-voice realization of the following figured basses.

EXERCISE 5   Harmonize the following melodies with a bass line and RNs (no inner voices), using standard harmonic patterns that correspond with the melodic patterns.

KEYBOARD HARMONY

1. Play and learn the progressions in example 4.10 of the textbook. Listen to the role of first-inversion chords in these elaborations of the I–V–I progression.

2. Play the following progressions in CM, GM, DM, and FM; and in Cm, Gm, Dm, and Am. You can also use them to practice harmonic dictation. A friend can play them in any order while you notate the bass and Roman numerals and recognize which one of the progressions is being played.

♪♪♪ Example 4.3

3. Soprano-bass patterns. Refer to example 4.9 in the textbook. Play the soprano-bass patterns in that example at the piano adding inner voices in keyboard texture, in the following major keys: C, G, D, and F; and in the following minor keys: C, G, D, and A.

4. Roman-numeral realization. To practice realization of Roman-numeral progressions, realize the following exercises at the piano, using keyboard texture: textbook, worksheet 4, exercise 3; and workbook, chapter 4, exercise 3.

5. Figured-bass realization. To practice realization of figured-bass progressions, realize the following exercises at the piano, using keyboard texture: textbook, worksheet 4, exercise 4; and workbook, chapter 4, exercise 4.

6. Melody harmonization. To practice melody harmonization, realize the following exercises at the piano, using keyboard texture: textbook, worksheet 4, exercise 6; and workbook, chapter 4, exercise 5.

Chapter 5

The Supertonic

EXERCISE 1   Analysis.

1. Analyze the opening phrase of Beethoven's Piano Concerto no. 4, III (example 5.1) with Roman numerals (RNs). What is the harmonic function of mm. 11–15? How does this phrase illustrate the close relationship between ii and IV?

♪♪♪ Example 5.1   L. v. Beethoven, Piano Concerto no. 4, op. 58, III, mm. 11–20 (piano part)

2. Analyze examples 5.2a, b, and c with Roman numerals.

Example 5.2a   J. S. Bach, Fugue no. 3 in C♯M, from *The Well-Tempered Clavier*, I

Example 5.2b   W. A. Mozart, Piano Sonata in B♭M, K. 333, I

Example 5.2c   W. A. Mozart, Sonata no. 18 for Violin and Piano, K. 56, III

EXERCISE 2   Realize the following progression in four voices. Remember to double-check the outer-voice frame for good first-species counterpoint.

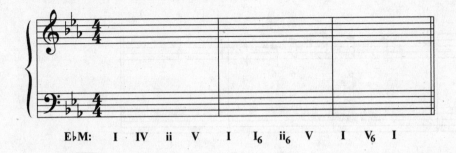

E♭M: I   IV   ii   V   I   I₆   ii₆   V   I   V₆   I

EXERCISE 3   Provide a RN analysis and realize in four voices. Remember to double-check the outer-voice frame for good first-species counterpoint.

Bm: 6   6   ♯   6   6   ♯   6

EXERCISE 4   *Melody harmonization*. Write a bass and RNs (no inner voices) harmonizing the following melodies. The harmonic rhythm (HR) is given.

1. Sing each melody several times before writing the harmonization.

2. Use only I, IV, or V in root position or first inversion.

3. First try to identify any melodic patterns that may be harmonized with some of the harmonic patterns you have learned.

4. Harmonize the notes marked with a 6 with first inversion triads. (If necessary, a 5 is used to indicate a root position triad.)

5. Check your two-voice contrapuntal frame to verify good voice leading.

6. Always *play your harmonizations* (as well as all your other exercises) before you turn them in. Make sure you are satisfied with them, and enjoy them!

EXERCISE 5   Harmonize the following melodies with a bass and RNs (no inner voices). Use I (i), IV (iv), V, or ii (ii°) in root position or first inversion. Remember to double-check the outer-voice frame for good first-species counterpoint.

DM:

HR:

KEYBOARD HARMONY

1. Play and learn the progressions in example 5.6 of the textbook. Listen to the role of both first-inversion chords and the supertonic in these elaborations of the I–V–I progression.

2. Play and learn the progressions in example 5.3 (in CM, DM, AM, and E♭M; play progressions 5.3c and also in Am, Bm, F♯m, and Cm), paying attention to the voice leading to and from the supertonic chords. Listen carefully to the progressions as you play them (or as a classmate plays them).

♪♪♪ Example 5.3

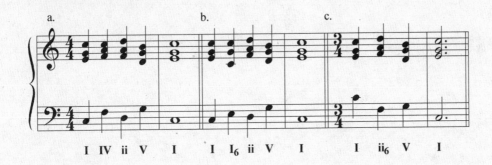

I IV ii V   I   I I₆ ii V   I   I ii₆ V   I

3. Soprano-bass patterns. Refer to example 5.5 in the textbook. Play the soprano-bass patterns in that example at the piano, adding inner voices in keyboard texture, in the same major and minor keys listed in keyboard exercise 2.

4. Roman-numeral and figured-bass realization. To practice realization of Roman-numeral and figured-bass progressions, realize the following exercises at the piano, using keyboard texture: textbook, worksheet 5, exercises 2 and 3; and workbook, chapter 5, exercises 2 and 3.

5. Melody harmonization. To practice melody harmonization, realize the following exercises at the piano, using keyboard texture: textbook, worksheet 5, exercises 4 and 5; and workbook, chapter 5, exercise 5.

Chapter 6

Nonchord Tones

EXERCISE 1 Analysis.

1. Identify and label all NCTs (nonchord tones) in the Corelli phrase reproduced in example 6.1. Besides the NCTs actually present in the melody, is any other NCT suggested by the figured bass?

2. Identify and label all the NCTs in anthology, no. 8 (Bach, Chorale 41), mm. 1–5.

3. Identify and label all the NCTs in anthology, no. 34 (Beethoven, Piano Sonata in Cm, op. 13, III), mm. 1–8. Because in this example the left hand arpeggiates chords, all the left-hand pitches may be interpreted as chord tones, with the only exceptions to be found in m. 1, beat 2 (notice the meter signature) and m. 3, beat 2. Identify the NCTs in these left-hand passages, besides the numerous NCTs throughout the right-hand melody.

Example 6.1   Archangelo Corelli, Sonata *La Folia,* op. 5, no. 12

EXERCISE 2   Add NCTs to the following chorale. Provide suspensions as required by the given figures. If you add simultaneous NCTs in different voices, make sure they are consonant among themselves. Be careful not to "overembellish"!

(Based on Bach, Chorale 27)

7-6   4-3   4-3

2-3 9-8 4-3   9-8 4-3

EXERCISE 3   Harmonize the given two-voice framework with i, iv, V, and their first inversions. First add inner voices. Then embellish the texture with NCTs.

Fm:

EXERCISE 4   Realize the following progression in four voices, including the suspensions indicated by the figures in the required voices.

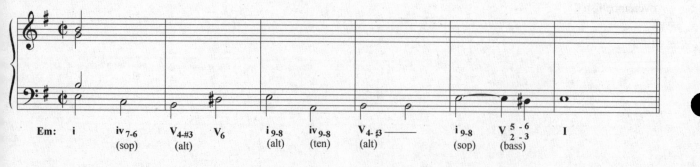

Em: i   iv 7-6   V 4-#3   V6   i 9-8   iv 9-8   V 4- #3 ——   i 9-8   V 5 - 6 2 - 3   I
          (sop)   (alt)   (alt)   (ten)   (alt)   (sop)   (bass)

EXERCISE 5   Complete the chain of 2–3 suspensions that has been started for you.

EXERCISE 6   Folk melodies often display a slow harmonic rhythm and numerous NCTs, as in the melodies reproduced below. Harmonize these melodies with a bass line and RNs (no inner voices). Use only I, ii, IV, V, and their first inversions. Note that for melodies a and b you will need to use V_7 in your harmonization. Sing, play, and sing again each of these melodies, and try to hear their harmonization as you play or sing. Be careful with the voice leading of your two-voice framework. For each melody, identify, mark, and label all NCTs.

Austria

b.

E♭M:
HR:

Germany

4. The following questions refer to example 7.3.

   a) What NCT is featured in the opening motive?

   b) Measures 5–6 are linear elaborations of the tonic triad. On the score, provide RNs for all the chords in these two measures. Explain here how each of the chords functions linearly to prolong the tonic harmony. How are the outer-voice pitches in m. 5 related linearly?

   c) What kind of cadence closes the first phrase (m. 8)?

   What kind of cadence closes the period?

   Explain the chords in mm. 15–16.

   d) How are the two "moving voices" in both hands related in mm. 1–4?

   By contrast, compare the *outer* voices in mm. 5–6. How is the contour of these voices designed in relation with each other?

   Finally, compare the contrapuntal motion in both hands in mm. 7–8. How are the melodic contours related in these measures?

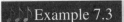 Example 7.3   L. v. Beethoven, Piano Sonata no. 9, op. 14, no. I, II, mm. 1–16

EXERCISE 2   Write the following triads in four voices with correct doubling.

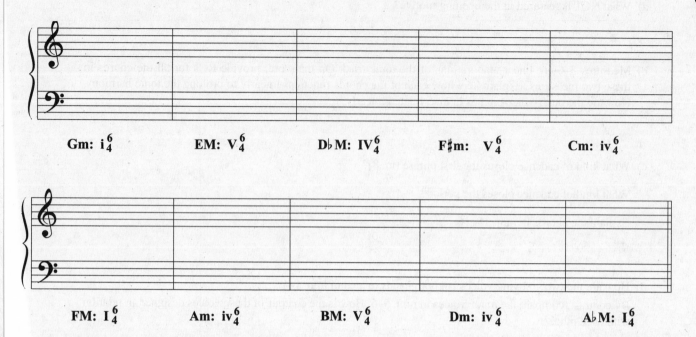

Gm: i$^6_4$ EM: V$^6_4$ D♭M: IV$^6_4$ F♯m: V$^6_4$ Cm: iv$^6_4$

FM: I$^6_4$ Am: iv$^6_4$ BM: V$^6_4$ Dm: iv$^6_4$ A♭M: I$^6_4$

EXERCISE 3   Realize the following short progressions in four voices. Provide RNs (Roman numerals) where needed.

a. Dm: i   N$^6_4$ i   b. EM: $^6_4$ c. FM: I   P$^6_4$ I$_6$ d. Em: 6   ♯$^6_4$

e. AM: IV   V$^{6-5}_{4-3}$ I   f. Gm: ii°$_6$ V$^{6-5}_{4-♯3}$ i   g. Bm: $^6_4$ ♯$^5_3$

EXERCISE 4   Realize the following progression in four voices. Provide RNs where needed. Remember to double-check the outer-voice frame for good first-species counterpoint.

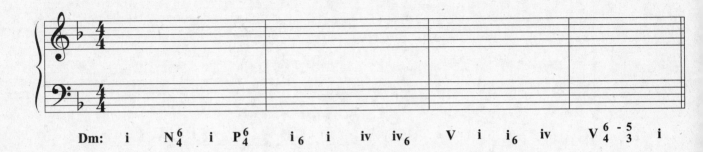

Dm: i   N⁶₄   i   P⁶₄   i₆   i   iv   iv₆   V   i   i₆   iv   V⁶₄ ⁻ ⁵₃   i

EXERCISE 5   Harmonize the following melody with a bass line and RNs (one chord per melody note). Include at least one of each of the following chords: passing ⁶₄, neighbor ⁶₄, cadential ⁶₄, and ii°₆ (besides i, iv, and V in root position or inversion).

Gm:

KEYBOARD HARMONY

1. Play and learn the progressions in example 7.12 of the textbook. Listen to the role of $^6_4$ chords in these elaborations of the I–V–I progression.

2. The following keyboard progressions contain all the $^6_4$ chord types studied in this chapter. Play and learn the progressions in CM, FM, B♭M, E♭M, and in their relative-minor keys: Am, Dm, Gm, and Cm.

Example 7.4

3. Soprano-bass patterns. Refer to example 7.13 in the textbook. Play the soprano-bass patterns in that example at the piano, adding inner voices in keyboard texture in the same major and minor keys listed in keyboard exercise 2.

4. Roman-numeral and figured-bass realization. To practice realization of Roman-numeral and figured-bass progressions, realize the following exercises at the piano, using keyboard texture: textbook, worksheet 7, exercises 3 and 4; and workbook, chapter 7, exercises 3 and 4.

5. Melody harmonization. To practice melody harmonization, realize the following exercises at the piano, using keyboard texture: textbook, worksheet 7, exercise 5; and workbook, chapter 7, exercise 5.

Chapter 8

The Dominant Seventh and Its Inversions

EXERCISE 1   Analysis. Refer to anthology, no. 20, Haydn, Sonata in DM.

1. Analyze mm. 9–15 with RNs (Roman numerals).

2. Measures 9–15 can be explained as a harmonic prolongation of I in FM. Explain the linear function of each chord and how it contributes to this extended prolongation.

3. Provide RNs for the chords in mm. 17–19. Explain their voice leading, noticing the resolution of any possible chordal dissonance.

EXERCISE 2   Write the following root position and inverted V_7 chords in four voices, and resolve each of them to the appropriate tonic chord. Write the key signature for each.

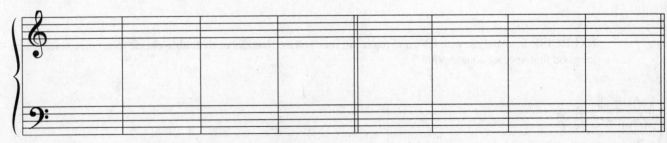

E♭M: V_7 AM: V_7 Gm: V_7 F♯m: V_7 Em: V_5^6 Dm: V_2^4 FM: V_3^4 Am: V_2^4

EXERCISE 3   Realize in four voices.

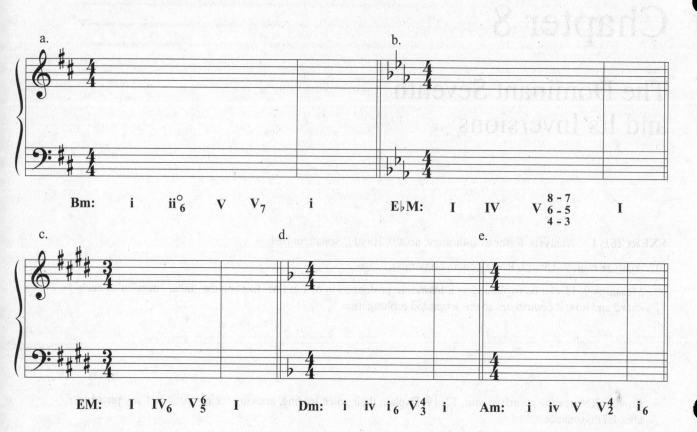

Bm: i   ii°₆   V   V₇   i

E♭M: I   IV   V $\begin{smallmatrix}8-7\\6-5\\4-3\end{smallmatrix}$ I

EM: I   IV₆   V$^6_5$ I

Dm: i   iv   i₆   V$^4_3$ i

Am: i   iv   V   V$^4_2$ i₆

EXERCISE 4   Provide correct RNs for the following bass. Include a passing $^6_4$ and one each of the three inversions of V₇.

EXERCISE 5   Analyze with RNs and realize in four voices. Remember to double-check your outer-voice frame for good first-species counterpoint.

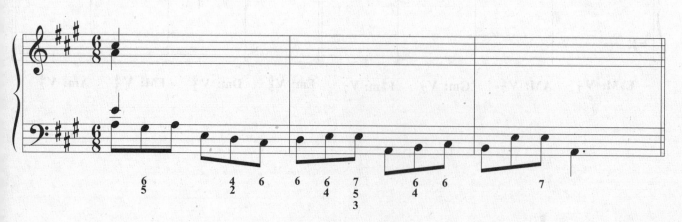

EXERCISE 6 Harmonize the following melody with a bass and RNs. Include as many dominant seventh chords (in root position or inversion) as possible. The harmonic rhythm is one chord per note, except for the two notes marked with a bracket, which will be harmonized with the same chord.

DM:

KEYBOARD HARMONY

1. Play and learn the progressions in example 8.12 of the textbook. Listen to the role of inverted dominant-seventh chords in these elaborations of the I–V–I progression.

2. Practice the keyboard progressions from example 8.1 in the following major keys: C, G, D, A, E, F, B♭, and A♭; and in the following minor keys: A, D, G, C, F, E, B, and F♯.

♪♪ Example 8.1

3. Soprano-bass patterns. Refer to examples 8.8 and 8.9 in the textbook. Play the soprano-bass patterns in those examples at the piano, adding inner voices in keyboard texture in the following major keys: C, G, D, A, and F; and in the following minor keys: A, D, G, C, and F.

4. Roman-numeral realization. To practice realization of Roman-numeral progressions, realize the following exercises at the piano, using keyboard texture: textbook, worksheet 8, exercises 4 and 6; and workbook, chapter 8, exercise 3.

5. Figured-bass realization. To practice realization of figured-bass progressions, realize the following exercises at the piano, using keyboard texture: textbook, worksheet 8, exercise 8; and workbook, chapter 8, exercise 5.

6. Melody harmonization. To practice melody harmonization, realize the following exercises at the piano, using keyboard texture: textbook, worksheet 8, exercise 9; and workbook, chapter 8, exercise 6.

Chapter 9

The Leading-Tone Triad

EXERCISE 1   Analysis.

1. a) Identify a leading-tone triad in each of the following examples: anthology, no. 20 (Haydn, Piano Sonata in DM), mm. 1–4; and anthology, no. 32 (Beethoven, Piano Sonata in Fm, op. 2, no. 1), mm. 1–8. Explain how each of these triads functions linearly, and comment on the voice leading used in their resolution.

   b) Analyze mm. 1–8 of the Beethoven example (anthology, no. 32) with RNs (Roman numerals), and explain how the initial tonic is prolonged through m.7 by linear means.

2. Analyze example 9.1 with RNs. Two areas extend I: mm. 21–23 prolong I and lead to the half cadence at m. 24. Then, mm. 25–30 again prolong I, leading to the final pre-dominant/dominant/tonic cadential pattern. On the score, indicate linear chords in these areas, showing their passing or neighbor function by means of a P or an N, respectively.

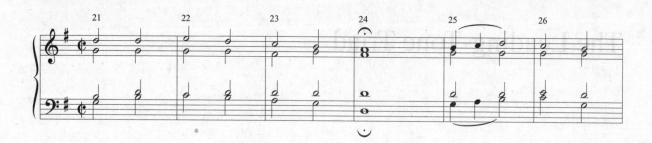

Example 9.1   R. Schumann, "Freue dich, o meine Seele," from *Album for the Young*, op. 68, mm. 21–32.

3. Example 9.2 shows mm. 3–6 of Bach's Chorale 96.
   a) Analyze mm. 3–4 with RNs.
   b) Circle and label all NCTs (nonchord tones).
   c) Measure 3, beats 3–4 and m. 4, beat 1, feature a progression studied in this chapter. What is unusual, in a minor key, with the chord in m. 3, beat 3? Why does Bach use this chord here? Could there be any melodic reasons that would preclude the use of the corresponding minor key chord?

Example 9.2   J. S. Bach, Chorale 96, "Jesu, meine Freude," mm. 3–6

EXERCISE 2   Analyze the following figured bass with RNs, and realize it in four voices. End the phrase with a
$\hat{5}$–#$\hat{6}$–#$\hat{7}$–$\hat{1}$ melodic fragment in the soprano. Remember to double-check your outer-voice frame for good first-
species counterpoint.

EXERCISE 3   Harmonize each of the following short melodic fragments in four voices. Write the bass and RNs
first, then fill in the inner voices. Use leading-tone triads for the notes marked with an asterisk.

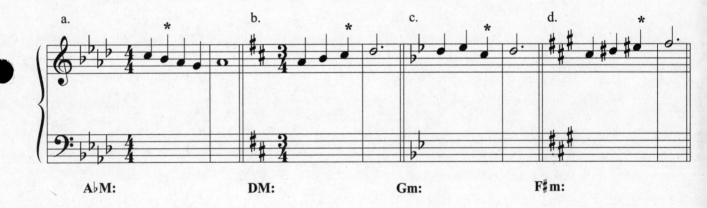

EXERCISE 4   Harmonize the following melody in four voices, with a correct chordal progression and good
voice leading. Harmonize all the soprano pitches as chord tones. Three of the pitches may be harmonized with
vii°$_6$, and for the rest you may use I, IV, ii, or V$_7$ in root position or inversion. Remember to double-check your
outer-voice frame for good first-species counterpoint.

KEYBOARD HARMONY

1. Play and learn the progressions in example 9.8 of the textbook.

2. Play the keyboard progressions in example 9.3 in a variety of keys as assigned by your instructor. Notice that example 9.3c can be played only in M if you want to avoid the $\flat\hat{6}$–$\sharp\hat{7}$ augmented 2nd. Example 9.3d provides a version of the same progression with $\hat{6}$ and $\hat{7}$ in different voices, suitable to be played in both M and m.

♪♪♪ Example 9.3

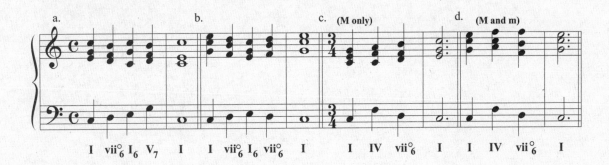

3. Soprano-bass patterns. Refer to example 9.7 in the textbook. Play the soprano-bass patterns in those examples at the piano, adding inner voices in keyboard texture in the keys assigned by your instructor.

4. Roman-numeral and figured-bass realization. To practice realization of Roman-numeral and figured-bass progressions, realize the following exercises at the piano, using keyboard texture: textbook, worksheet 9, exercises 2 and 3; and workbook, chapter 9, exercise 2.

5. Melody harmonization. To practice melody harmonization, realize the following exercises at the piano, using keyboard texture: textbook, worksheet 9, exercise 4; and workbook, chapter 9, exercises 3 and 4.

Chapter 10

Cadences

EXERCISE 1   Analysis. Study and label each of the following cadences. Name the cadence type, and list specific RNs (Roman numerals) and other characteristics to justify your choice.

1. Anthology, no. 52, Verdi, *La traviata*:
   Measures 31–32:

   Measures 41–42:

2. Anthology, no. 19, Haydn, Minuet, m. 8.

3. Anthology, no. 31, Paradis, *Sicilienne*:
   Measures 3–4:

   Measures 27–28:

4. Anthology, no. 28, Mozart, Piano Sonata in B♭M, III, m. 76.

5. Example 10.1.

6. Example 10.2.

7. Example 10.3.
   Measures 19–20:

   Measures 20–22:

8. Example 10.4.

♪♪ Example 10.1   George Frideric Handel, "Hallelujah," from *Messiah,* closing measures

-lu - jah,   Hal - le - lu - jah,   Hal - le - lu - jah,   Hal - le   -   lu   -   jah.

-lu - jah,   Hal - le - lu - jah,   Hal - le - lu - jah,   Hal   le   -   lu   -   jah.

-lu - jah,   Hal - le - lu - jah,   Hal - le - lu - jah,   Hal   le   -   lu   -   jah.

-lu - jah,   Hal - le - lu - jah,   Hal - le - lu - jah,   Hal   le   lu   -   jah.

♪♪ Example 10.2   J. S. Bach, Chorale 143, *In dulci jubilo,* mm. 20–24

Dm:

CAD:

♪♪♪ Example 10.3   Robert Schumann, "Ich will meine Seele tauchen," from *Dichterliebe*, op. 48, no. 5

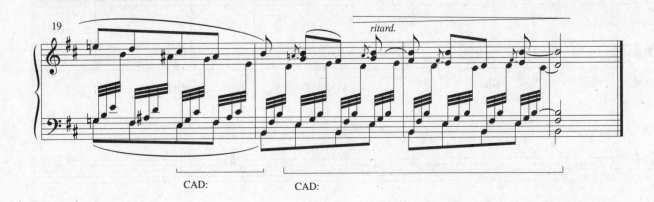

CAD: CAD:

♪♪♪ Example 10.4   J. S. Bach, Invention no. 4 in Dm, mm. 46–52

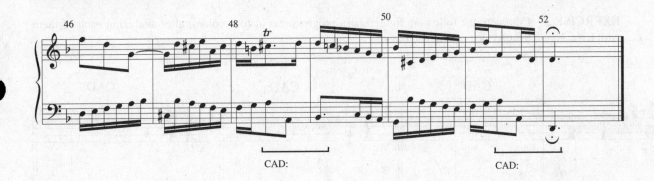

CAD: CAD:

EXERCISE 2   Realize the following cadences in four voices as required. Some soprano melodic patterns are provided, and so are some Roman numerals. Provide RNs where missing.

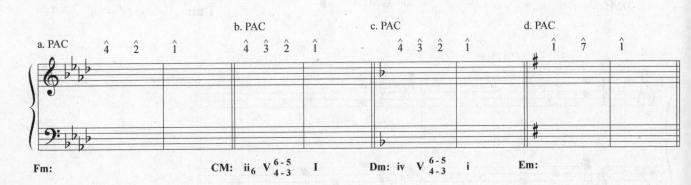

EXERCISE 3   Complete the following figured bass progressions in four voices, after analyzing each of them with RNs. Name the cadence type in each case.

EXERCISE 4   Provide a RN analysis for the following bass, using any of the chords we have studied so far, in root position or inversion.

AM:

EXERCISE 5

1. Harmonize exercise 5a in four voices (bass, RNs, inner voices). Name the cadences. Remember: what you are writing *is music*. Listen to it, make sure it sounds good, and enjoy *both* writing and playing it.

2. Harmonize exercise 5b with bass and RNs (no inner voices). Name the cadences. Remember to double-check this outer-voice frame for good first-species counterpoint.

KEYBOARD HARMONY

1. Play the following progressions, in the following keys: CM, Am, GM, Em, DM, Bm, FM, Dm, B♭M, and Gm. Learn to recognize the various cadential formulas aurally as you play them, and do aural recognition drills with a friend.

♪♪♪ Example 10.5

2. Cadential patterns. Realize at the piano the cadential patterns outlined in the following exercises: textbook, worksheet 10, exercise 2; and workbook, chapter 10, exercise 2.

3. Roman-numeral realization. To practice realization of Roman-numeral progressions, realize the following exercises at the piano, using keyboard texture: textbook, worksheet 10, exercises 3 and 4.

4. Figured-bass realization. To practice realization of figured-bass progressions, realize the following exercises at the piano, using keyboard texture: textbook, worksheet 10, exercise 5; and workbook, chapter 10, exercise 3.

5. Melody harmonization. To practice melody harmonization, realize the following exercises at the piano, using keyboard texture: workbook, chapter 10, exercises 5a and b.

Chapter 11

Melodic Organization I: Phrase Structure

EXERCISE 1   Analysis. Study the phrase/period structure of the following examples. For each of the examples, provide a brief discussion of structure, including at least the following information:

1. Is the fragment based on a motive?

2. How many phrases are there? Provide measure numbers and phrase numbers for each. Are any phrases connected by elision?

3. Identify the cadences at the end of each phrase. In cases where only a melody is given, you can identify cadences on the basis of the given Roman numerals and the cadential melodic gestures.

4. Is there any antecedent-consequent phrase structure?

5. What kind of a period is this? One or several of the following may apply to each example: parallel, contrasting, symmetrical, asymmetrical, three-phrase (or four-phrase), double, modulating, phrase group (not a period).

6. Provide a line (bubble) diagram for each of the examples, indicating the following items: phrases/measure numbers; phrase relationship with letters; cadences at the end of each phrase (with a cadence-type abbreviation); and long-range harmonic motion from beginning to end of each phrase.

Examples for analysis:

1. Anthology, no. 22, Chevalier de Saint–Georges, Violin Concerto.

   Discussion:

   Form diagram:

2. Anthology, no. 6, Minuet from *Notebook for Anna Magdalena Bach,* mm. 1–16.

   Discussion:

   Form diagram:

3. Example 11.1.

   Discussion:

   Form diagram:

Example 11.1   Amy Beach, *Sweetheart, Sigh No More,* op. 14, no. 3, mm. 3–13

It was with doubt and trem-bling   I   whis-pered   in her ear.   Go, take her an-swer,

I   **V₇   I**

bird-on-bough,   That all the world   may   hear   Sweet-heart,   sigh   no   more!

V₇   **(I)**   **V₇**   **V₇   I**

4. Anthology, no. 32, Beethoven, Piano Sonata in Fm, op. 2, no. 1, III, Menuetto, mm. 1–14.

   Discussion:

   Form diagram:

5. Anthology, no. 32, Beethoven, Piano Sonata in Fm, op. 2, no. 1, III, Trio, mm. 41–50

   Discussion:

   Form diagram:

---

6. Notate (rhythm only) the most characteristic melodic rhythmic motive in:
   a) Anthology, no. 6, Minuet from *Notebook for A. M. Bach.*

   b) Anthology, no. 19, Haydn, Minuet.

   c) Anthology, no. 26, Mozart, Piano Sonata in CM, III.

7. In anthology, no. 19 (Haydn, Minuet), the combination of rhythmic motive, phrasing, and harmonic resolution create a series of elisions in mm. 1–4. Given the rhythm of these measures in example 11.2, show the phrasing of the motives with brackets (there will be three of them), indicating clearly where the elisions occur (see example 11.3 in the book for a model).

Example 11.2

EXERCISE 2   Write a melody in antecedent-consequent form (a parallel period). The beginning is given. Be ready to sing or play your melody if asked to by your instructor.

Vivace

GM:

EXERCISE 3   Write a melody with the following characteristics: four phrases (double period), form a₁–b₁–a₂–b₂, sixteen measures long. Indicate what cadences are implied at the end of each phrase. Be musical, and be able to sing what you write.

EM:

EXERCISE 4   Analyze the following progression with RNs, and realize in four voices.

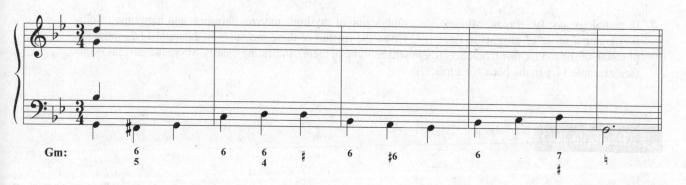

Gm:

EXERCISE 5   Harmonize the following melody with a bass and RNs, a chord per note. Use the chordal inversions indicated by the figures. Label the cadences at the end of each phrase. Remember to double-check this outer-voice frame for good first-species counterpoint.

Chapter 12

Melodic Organization II: Thematic Development; Phrase Extension

EXERCISE 1   Analysis. Identify and name the technique(s) of thematic development in the following examples. In the case of sequences, identify the exact type.

1. Anthology, no. 26, Mozart, Piano Sonata in CM, III, mm. 16–17.

2. Example 12.1.
   a) Explain the relationship between m. 8 and 9.

   b) Between mm. 11–12 and 13–14.

   c) Between mm. 7 and 19,

   d) How is the three-note motive transformed in mm. 15–18?

   e) How do we call the rhythmic relationship created by the three-note motive against the $\frac{3}{4}$ meter?

Example 12.1   Edvard Grieg, "Anitra's Dance", from *Peer Gynt*, Suite I, op. 46, III mm. 7–22

3. Example 12.2. How is fragment b related to fragment a?

Example 12.2   J. S. Bach, Fugue no. 9 in EM, from *The Well-Tempered Clavier*, II

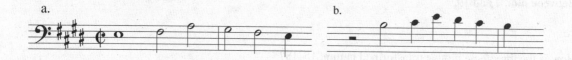

4. Example 12.3. How is fragment b related to fragment a?

Example 12.3   J. S. Bach, Fugue no. 8 in D♯m, from *The Well-Tempered Clavier*, II

5. Example 12.4. How is fragment b related to fragment a?

Example 12.4   Guillaume Dufay, *Missa L'Homme armé*, "Agnus Dei"

6. Example 12.5. How is fragment b related to fragment a?

Example 12.5   Ludwig van Beethoven, Sonata op. 26, I

7. Anthology, no. 28, Mozart, Piano Sonata in B♭M, III, mm. 16–20.

8. Refer to anthology, no. 33, Beethoven, Piano Sonata in Cm, op. 10, no. 1, II. Explain the techniques of formal growth in mm. 1–8.

9. Refer to anthology, no. 27, Mozart, Sonata in AM, Theme. In previous chapters we discussed various aspects of this piece's formal organization. As a summary and further study of the piece, provide a complete formal analysis (of the complete theme, that is, mm. 1–18) in the form of a brief, but clear and well-organized, analytical paper. Turn in an annotated copy of the score, on which you will mark the following information, which you should also cover in your paper:

a) Circle the main motive of the piece.

b) Are there any prominent rhythmic motives in this fragment? What are they?

c) Mark with brackets (one per segment) all the sequences in the piece.

d) Label and number the phrases (phrase 1, phrase 2, etc.).

e) Are the two phrase members of phrase 1 (mm. 1–4) similar or contrasting?

f) How many periods are there?

g) Mark and label all the cadences in the piece.

h) Could the piece have ended in m. 16?

i) What is the formal function of mm. 17–18?

j) Provide a line diagram of the complete piece, indicating phrases, periods, cadences (with abbreviations and RNs), measure numbers, and letters to indicate form.

10. Discuss the techniques of thematic (melodic) development in anthology, no. 32, Beethoven, op. 2, no. 1, I, mm. 1–20. Notice specifically the following relationships, and provide exact terms:

   a) Measures 1–2 with 3–4:

   b) Measures 5–6 with 1–2:

   c) Measure 6 with m. 5:

   d) Measures 11–14 with 1–2:

   e) Measures 15–16 and following (to m. 20):

EXERCISE 2   Write extended or varied versions of the following melody using the devices specified in each case. Be austere in your versions (do not try to vary or add too much; only what is necessary to make good musical sense). Make sure that your versions are musical, and that you are satisfied with them.

   a. Repetition

   b. Variation (rhythmic, or pitch and rhythm)

   c. Sequence

d. Change of mode

e. Interpolation by fragmentation

f. Intervallic expansion or contraction

g. Cadential extension

h. Augmentation

i. Inversion (begin on pitch B)

j. Retrograde

EXERCISE 3

1. Complete the following parallel period with a consequent.

2. After you write your consequent, and using your own music paper, write four more versions of the same consequent, using the following extensions in each of them. Think musically, and write extensions that you think make good musical sense in the context of this period.

   a) An interpolation using fragmentation and sequence.

   b) An interpolation using repetition and variation.

   c) An interpolation using new melodic material.

   d) A cadential extension.

EXERCISE 4   Provide a RN analysis and realize in four voices.

Chapter 13

Harmonic Rhythm; Metric Reduction

EXERCISE 1 Analysis.

1. In the spaces below, diagram the harmonic rhythm (HR) for each of the following examples. For each of these examples, indicate also whether the HR is very slow, slow, fast, regular, irregular, and/or accelerating toward a cadence.

    a) Anthology, no. 26, Mozart, Piano Sonata in CM, K. 309, III, mm. 1–19.

    b) Anthology, no. 32, Beethoven, Piano Sonata in Fm, op. 2, no. 1, I, mm. 1–20.

    c) Anthology, no. 32, Beethoven, Piano Sonata in Fm, op. 2, no. 1, I, mm. 140–152.

    d) Anthology, no. 33, Beethoven, Piano Sonata in Cm, op. 10, no. 1, II, mm. 1–8.

2. *Metric and harmonic accents.* Provide diagrams of HR along with symbols of strong and weak metric accent for each of the following examples. Discuss briefly how metric and harmonic accents correlate. How are V and I chords placed metrically? Is there any clear conflict between metric and harmonic accents?

    a) Anthology, no. 50, Schumann, "Folk Song."

b) Anthology, no. 33, Beethoven, Piano Sonata in Cm, op. 10, no. 1, II, mm. 1–8.

3. Analyze example 13.1 with Roman numerals (RNs), and provide weak/strong metric symbols above each beat in the score. Then, discuss briefly in the space below the relationship between metric and harmonic accents, focusing on metric placement for the different harmonic functions and for the chord successions implying a tension-release progression.

♪♪♪ Example 13.1   J. S. Bach, Chorale 22, "Schmücke dich, o liebe Seele," mm. 1–5

EXERCISE 2   Metric reduction. Provide a metric reduction of anthology, no. 34 (Beethoven, Piano Sonata in Cm, op. 13, III), mm. 1–8.

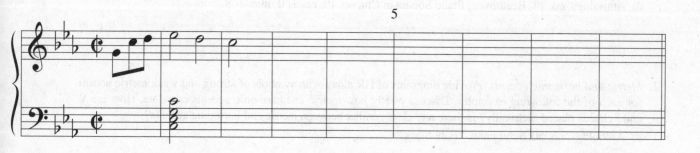

EXERCISE 3   Example 13.2 features a compound melody. In the staff below it, renotate the passage clearly showing the various voices that make up the compound melody. Refer to examples 13.9 and 13.10 in the textbook for models of notation.

Example 13.2   J. S. Bach, Brandenburg Concerto no. 6, III, mm. 1–8

EXERCISE 4   *Writing harmonic progressions.* Be careful with the correlation of metric and harmonic accents, and write harmonic phrases that are logical and musical. Play your progressions and make sure you like them!

1. Write a progression (bass and RNs only) in DM, in $\frac{4}{4}$, using only I, IV, and V, and their first inversions.

DM:

2. Write a progression in B♭M, in $\frac{3}{4}$, including a passing $^6_4$ and a V^4_2, besides any of the other chords we have already studied.

B♭M:

3. Write a progression in Fm, in $\frac{2}{4}$, including a deceptive resolution of V, a cadential $^6_4$, and a plagal cadence, besides any of the other chords we have already studied.

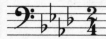

Fm:

4. Write a progression in Bm, in $\frac{6}{8}$, using a vii°^{6}, a neighbor $^6_4$, and a V^6_5, besides i, iv, V, or ii in root position or inversion.

Bm:

Chapter 14

The Mediant, Submediant, and Subtonic Triads

EXERCISE 1   Analysis.

1. The cadence marked with a bracket in example 14.1 appears to be a PAC (perfect authentic cadence) in Bm. Examine it closely, and comment on the exact type of cadence this is and on the chords involved in it.

♪♪♪ Example 14.1   J. S. Bach, Air, from Orchestral Suite no. 3, BWV 1068, m. 10

Bm:

2. a) How is I in CM prolonged in mm. 41–43 of Example 14.2? Explain exactly what chords are used by Brahms in these measures, and how they function.

   b) In m. 44 the bass seems to indicate a dominant harmony. Is the chord throughout the measure a plain V, or is the dominant harmony elaborated in any way?

c) This passage is in $\frac{6}{8}$. How does Brahms alter your perception of this meter? What metric ambiguities can you identify, considering phrasing, rhythmic accents, and grouping?

Example 14.2   Johannes Brahms, Intermezzo in CM, op. 119, no. 3, mm. 41–45

3. a) Analyze mm. 1–4 of anthology, no. 24 (Mozart, DM Sonata) with RNs (Roman numerals). What is the function of vi in this phrase?

   b) Analyze mm. 9–12 of anthology, no. 28 (Mozart, B♭M Sonata) with RNs. What is the function of vi in this phrase? How does the harmonization of this phrase compare with the one you just analyzed in the DM Sonata? What kind of NCTs (nonchord tones) are featured in m. 11?

   c) Refer to anthology, no. 19 (Haydn, Divertimento in CM, Trio), and explain the resolution of the dominant of E♭M in mm. 31–32.

4. a) Analyze mm. 1–10 in example 14.3 with RNs.
      Questions b to h refer to mm. 1–10.

b) vi is used to prolong the tonic twice in this passage. In what measures?

c) How is the dominant prolonged linearly in m. 7? How is it resolved to m. 8 and why?

d) This passage is mainly harmonized using descending 5th root motions. Mark every root progression of 5th in the example with brackets. (Notice that some of these root progressions appear in first inversion. Mark them anyway.)

e) This passage is based on two melodic motives. Circle all appearances of both motives and label them with a 1 or a 2. How is each of these motives characteristic (and immediately recognizable), and how do they contrast from one another?

f) Do the motives appear in literal transpositions every time they are repeated, or are they varied somehow? How?

g) Are mm. 8–9 related to any of the two motives? How?

h) Describe the texture in mm. 1–10. What is the role of each line?

i) How do the texture and the roles of instruments change in mm. 11–25?

j) How is motive 2 treated in mm. 15–17? Be very specific, and circle in these measures the pitches from the original motives in mm. 5–7.

k) On what kind of cadence does the passage close?

l) What is the function of the bass in mm. 20–25? Use the exact term (which you learned in chapter 6).

Example 14.3   L. v. Beethoven, Sonata for Violin and Piano, op. 24 (*Spring*), I, mm. 1–25

EXERCISE 5   Harmonize the following melody with a bass line and RNs, using the given HR (harmonic rhythm). Include the following chords in your harmonization: III, vii°₆, a deceptive resolution of V, a cadential $^6_4$, and a plagal cadence at the end.

Em:
HR:

EXERCISE 6   Harmonize the following melodies with RNs and write a keyboard realization of your harmonization. You should begin by determining the correct HR for each melody, taking into account any possible NCTs. Use any of the chords we have studied so far.

a.   **Moderato**

Cm:

b.   **Allegro vivo**   Britai

DM:

EXERCISE 7

1. Write progressions (bass and RNs) using the chords indicated in each case, in the required meters.

    a) iii, vi, V$_3^4$

    b) vii°$_6$, a deceptive resolution of V

    c) VII, III, V$_2^4$, a cadential $_4^6$

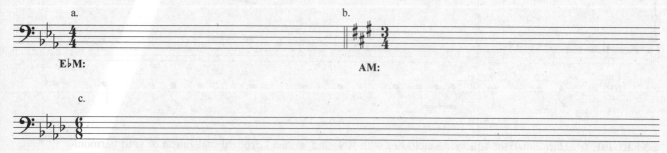

2. Choose one of your own progressions from above, and use it as a harmonic basis to compose a phrase for a melodic instrument of your choice (such as flute, clarinet in B♭, violin, etc.) and keyboard accompaniment. Your phrase should consist of a simple melody (for the melodic instrument) with a keyboard-style accompaniment (both hands).

KEYBOARD HARMONY

1. Play and learn the progressions in example 14.15 of the textbook. Listen to the role of the mediant, submediant, and subtonic chords in these elaborations of the I–V–I progression.

2. Play the keyboard progressions in example 14.4 in the keys assigned by your instructor. (Suggested keys: CM, AM, EM, E♭M, A♭M; and Am, F♯m, C♯m, Cm, and Fm)

Example 14.4

3. Soprano-bass patterns. Refer to examples 14.12, 14.13, and 14.14 in the textbook. Play the soprano-bass patterns in that example at the piano, adding inner voices in keyboard texture, in the same major and minor keys suggested previously in exercise 2.

4. Roman-numeral and figured-bass realization. To practice realization of Roman-numeral and figured-bass progressions, realize the following exercises at the piano, using keyboard texture: textbook, worksheet 14, exercises 2 and 4; and workbook, chapter 14, exercises 2 and 3.

5. Melody harmonization. To practice melody harmonization, realize the following exercises at the piano, using keyboard texture: textbook, worksheet 14, exercise 5; and workbook, chapter 14, exercises 5 and 6.

Chapter 15

Other Diatonic Seventh Chords

EXERCISE 1   Analysis.

1. Study mm. 1–12 of anthology, no. 47, Schumann, "Ich grolle nicht."

   a) Provide RNs (Roman numerals) for mm. 1–9. Notice that the first chord in m. 3, which we studied in this chapter, actually belongs to Cm because of the A♭ (♭$\hat{6}$). Assign it the same RN you would in Cm, and think of it as a chord "borrowed" from the minor mode. Do not assign a RN to the second chord in m. 4, but rather explain how it functions linearly.

   b) What is the underlying progression (think of downbeat chords for each measure) in mm. 4–9? Think of both root progression and chordal progression. Then, how do the "upbeat" chords in each measure function?

   c) Think of mm. 9–12 as an extended V_7–I progression. How are the V_7 at m. 9 and the I at m. 12 connected linearly? Think first of the bass motion from $\hat{5}$ to $\hat{1}$. Then look also at the piano's top voice, moving down from $\hat{2}$ to $\hat{3}$. How would the term "wedge" apply to this contrapuntal gesture?

   d) 1) In which ways is the melody unified—motivically? rhythmically? other?

2) The words mean: "I hold no resentment, and even if my heart breaks, O love forever lost, I hold no resentment." How is the heartbreak ("Herz") expressed and intensified musically?

How is the concept of love lost (and the subsequent feeling of grief) expressed (think, for instance, of the bass line on the words "ewig verlornes Lieb," but also of how the singer expresses the loss: Where is the climactic high point of the fragment?)?

What bass motion accompanies the final two statements of "ich grolle nicht"? If this contour, as opposed to the bass line in mm. 4–9, shows some hope, is the feeling confirmed by the lines in both the voice and the piano's right hand in mm. 9–12?

2. How does Paradis prolong the tonic in mm. 6–8 of example 15.1? What standard cadential formula (including the predominant chord—do not overlook the vocal line) does she use?

♪♪♪ Example 15.1   Maria Theresia von Paradis, "Morgenlied eines armen Mannes," mm. 6–10

EXERCISE 4   Harmonize the following melody with a keyboard texture. Include two leading-tone seventh chords, a deceptive progression, and a cadential 4–3 suspension.

FM:

HR:

EXERCISE 5

1. Harmonize the following melody and realize the harmonization for keyboard. A harmonic rhythm is suggested. You may want to take advantage of the possibility to use neighbor $^6_4$ chords in mm. 1–2, and a V_7 in m. 3.

2. After you write your harmonization, circle and label all NCTs (nonchord tones) in the melody. Also, identify all the sequences in the melody and mark each sequence segment with a bracket.

DM:

HR:

Italy

EXERCISE 6

1. Write progressions (bass and RNs) in the keys and meters indicated below. Use the following chords (in any order, but correctly resolved):

   a) $vii^{\emptyset}_7$, IV^6_5, ii^6_5

   b) $vii^{\circ6}_5$, iv_7, $vii^{\circ4}_2$

   c) ii^4_2, $vii^{\circ4}_3$, ii_7

a.   b.

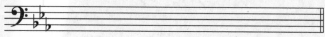

DM: Fm:

c.

E♭M:

2. Choose one of your own progressions from above, and use it as a harmonic basis to compose a phrase for a melodic instrument of your choice (such as flute, clarinet in B♭, violin) and keyboard accompaniment. Your phrase should consist of a simple melody (for the melodic instrument) with a keyboard-style accompaniment (both hands).

KEYBOARD HARMONY

1. Play and learn the progressions in examples 15.19 and 15.20 of the textbook. Listen to the role of seventh chords in these elaborations of the I–V–I progression.

2. Play the keyboard progressions in example 15.3 in a variety of M and m keys, as assigned by your instructor. (Suggested keys: CM, GM, DM, AM, EM, FM, B♭M, E♭M, A♭M; and their relative minor keys.)

♪♪♪ Example 15.3

3. Soprano-bass patterns. Refer to examples 15.17 and 15.18 in the textbook. Play the soprano-bass patterns in that example at the piano, adding inner voices in keyboard texture, in the same major and minor keys suggested in exercise 2.

4. Roman-numeral realization. To practice realization of Roman-numeral progressions, realize the following exercises at the piano, using keyboard texture: textbook, worksheet 15, exercises 3 and 4; and workbook, chapter 15, exercise 2.

5. Figured-bass realization. To practice realization of figured-bass progressions, realize the following exercise at the piano, using keyboard texture: workbook, chapter 15, exercise 3.

6. Melody harmonization. To practice melody harmonization, realize the following exercises at the piano, using keyboard texture: textbook, worksheet 15, exercise 5; and workbook, chapter 15, exercises 4 and 5.

Chapter 16

Harmonic Sequences

EXERCISE 1   Analysis

1. The following examples are based on harmonic sequences. Identify the exact type of sequence for each example, including root motion (by 5ths, 3rds, 2nds, etc.), position of chords, and specific voice-leading patterns for each sequence.

> Example 16.1a   A. Corelli, "Corrente," from *Sonata da camera a tre*, op. 4, no. 11, mm. 20–24

Example 16.1b   Jean Marie Leclair, Sonata for Two Violins, op. 3, no. 2, III, mm. 33–40

Example 16.1c   W. A. Mozart, Piano Concerto in AM, K. 488, I, mm. 259–60

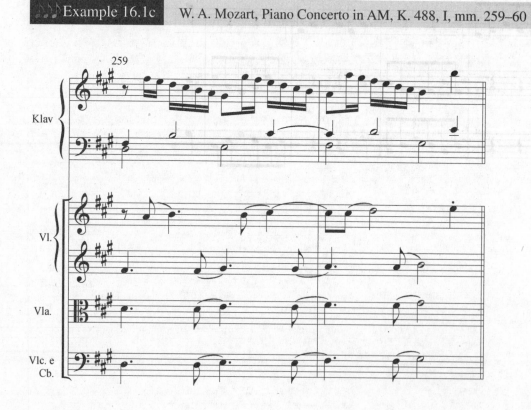

2. a) Analyze and compare the three phrases in example 16.2. Refer back to example 13.8 in the textbook (Bach's "Chaconne" for violin) and read the commentary after that example. Now consider the bass in the three phrases of example 16.2 (in examples 16.2a and b, consider only the downbeat of each measure). What kind of bass is this? How is this piece similar to the Bach fragment in example 13.8?

   b) What is the common underlying progression in both examples 16.2a and b (consider chord roots)? What is the compositional principle (the element of formal growth) in all three phrases?

   c) Compare example 16.2a to the paradigms in examples 16.5 and 16.6 in the textbook. Can you see any voice-leading relationships between this phrase and one or more of the paradigms?

   Now do the same comparison for example 16.2b.

   Finally, what basic harmonic/voice-leading technique can you identify in example 16.2c? Consider only the left hand, and you will find two separate and familiar voice-leading patterns—one of them taking into account the second eighth note in each measure and its motion to the half note, and the other one considering the suspension figure and its resolution to the half note.

♩♪♪ **Example 16.2**   G. F. Handel, "Chaconne," from *Trois Leçons*, mm. 89–92, 105–109, and 113–117

♪♪♪ Example 16.2   Continued

c. Var. 14.

3. Play and analyze the progressions in the keyboard part of example 16.3. Notice the basic two-measure harmonic rhythm, although you should pay attention for possible chordal alterations in the second measure of each harmony. What is the underlying root progression? Are any seventh chords used, and how? What is the structure of the melody this progression harmonizes?

♪♪♪ Example 16.3   Fritz Kreisler, *Liebesleid*, mm. 1–16

4. a) Examine mm. 25–27 of example 16.4. What is the type of progression? What kind of voice-leading paradigm do you recognize (refer to the paradigms studied in chapter 16)?

   b) Compare mm. 25–27 with 30–32. How is the latter progression different from the former? Analyze the chords and voice leading in mm. 30–32 carefully.

   c) The passage closes with a cadential pedal on $\hat{1}$ prolonging a I chord (mm. 32–36). Assume for now that all of m. 32 is a I chord, with a prolonging passing-tone F on beat 2. What are the other two chords used on the pedal (mm. 33 and 35)?

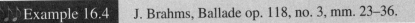

Example 16.4   J. Brahms, Ballade op. 118, no. 3, mm. 23–36.

EXERCISE 2

1. Write a complete circle of 5ths in four voices.

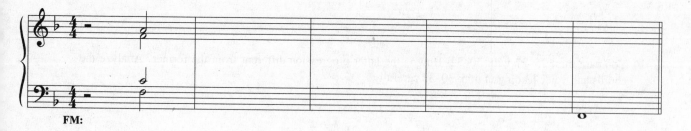

FM:

2. a) Write a diatonic seventh circle of 5ths in four voices.

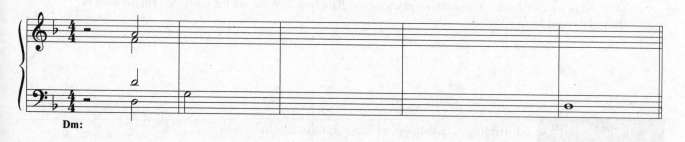

Dm:

b) On your own music paper, write a second version of this progression for piano, and compose a melody on it.

3. Realize the following sequence of parallel $\frac{6}{3}$ chords.

B♭M: 6   6   6   6   5

4. Realize the progression in four voices. Notice that it combines three sequential paradigms we have studied in this chapter. Realize the sequences following your models in the textbook (examples 16.6 and 16.17), and be very careful with doublings and faulty parallel 8ves or 5ths.

FM: 6   6   7-6   7-6   7-6   5-6   5-6   5-6   5-6

EXERCISE 3   On your own music paper, realize the following harmonic sequences in four voices (three $\frac{4}{4}$ measures each).

1. A root-position circle of 5ths with a 10–10–10–10 outer-voice paradigm, in Cm.

2. A circle of 5ths alternating root-position and first-inversion chords, with a 6–5–6–5 outer-voice paradigm, in GM.

3. A sequence descending by steps using the 7–6 technique, in CM.

4. A sequence by descending 3rds with interpolated $\frac{5}{3}$ chords (with a bass pattern "down a 4th—up a 2nd"), in Bm.

KEYBOARD HARMONY   Play and learn all the sequences in example 16.20 in the textbook in CM, GM, and FM, and in Cm, Gm, and Fm.

PART 2

*Chromatic Harmony
and Form*

Chapter 17

Secondary Dominants I

EXERCISE 1   Analysis.

1. Refer to anthology, no. 34 (Beethoven, Sonata in Cm, op. 13, III), mm. 12–16. What chord is tonicized twice in these measures? Provide a RN (Roman numeral) analysis for this complete passage.

2. What secondary dominant can you identify in example 17.1, m. 18, beat 4? And in m. 20, beat 1? Provide exact RNs for each.

> ♪♪ Example 17.1   J. S. Bach, Chorale 107, "Herzlich lieb hab'ich dich, o Herr," mm. 16–21

3. Example 17.2 presents a clear prolongation of the tonic chord. Explain. How is it prolonged? Are chromaticism and tonicization part of this prolongation? Which degree is tonicized, and how?

Example 17.2   W. A. Mozart, Piano Quartet in E♭M, K. 493, I, mm. 1–5

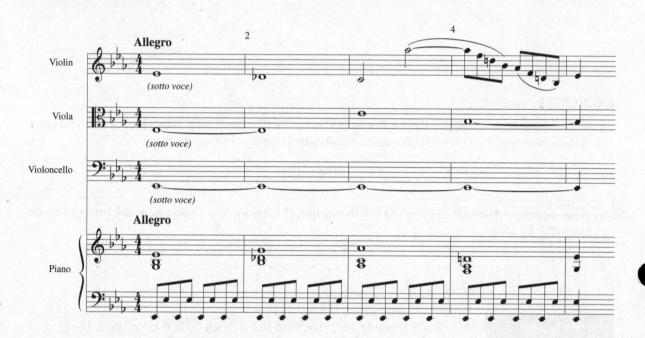

4. Example 17.3 begins with a secondary dominant. Provide RNs for the complete example. Does it feature any other tonicization? When is the tonic clearly established?

Example 17.3   L. v. Beethoven, Symphony no. 1 in CM, op. 21, I, mm. 1–6

EXERCISE 6

1. Write your own progressions (bass and RNs) in the keys and meters indicated below. Use the required chords, besides any of the other chords we have already studied. Make sure you resolve secondary dominants (and any other chords that require resolution) correctly.

   a) F#m; include V_2^4/iv, ii$^{\varnothing6}_5$, V_5^6/V, and a cad. $^6_4$.
   b) GM; include V_7/IV and V_3^4/V.

a.

F#m:

b.

GM:

2. Choose one of your own progressions from above, and use it as a harmonic basis to compose a phrase for a melodic instrument and keyboard accompaniment.

KEYBOARD HARMONY

1. Play and learn the progressions in examples 17.13, 17.14, and 17.15 of the textbook. Listen to the role of secondary dominants in these elaborations of the I–V–I progression.

2. Play the keyboard progressions in example 17.4 in a variety of M and m keys, as assigned by your instructor. (Suggested keys: CM, Cm, GM, Gm, DM, Dm, FM, Fm, B♭M, B♭m, D♭M, C#m)

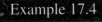

Example 17.4

3. Soprano-bass patterns. Refer to examples 17.11 and 17.12 in the textbook. Play the soprano-bass patterns in that example at the piano, adding inner voices in keyboard texture in the same major and minor keys suggested in exercise 2.

4. Roman-numeral realization. To practice realization of Roman-numeral progressions, realize the following exercises at the piano, using keyboard texture: textbook, worksheet 17, exercises 3, 4, and 5; and workbook, chapter 17, exercises 2 and 3.

5. Figured-bass realization. To practice realization of figured-bass progressions, realize the following exercise at the piano, using keyboard texture: workbook, chapter 17, exercise 4.

6. Melody harmonization. To practice melody harmonization, realize the following exercises at the piano, using keyboard texture: textbook, worksheet 17, exercise 6; and workbook, chapter 17, exercise 5.

Chapter 18

Secondary Dominants II

EXERCISE 1 Analysis.

1. Refer back to example 17.1 (Bach, Chorale 107). We have already identified tonicizations of IV and V in the last phrase of this example. What degree is tonicized at the end of the first phrase (m. 16, fermata)? And what other degree is immediately tonicized at the beginning of the second phrase (m. 16, beat 4 to m. 17, beat 1)? Provide RNs (Roman numerals) for both tonicizations.

2. Provide RNs for the tonicization in mm. 2–3 of example 18.1.

> **Example 18.1**   Anton Bruckner, Symphony no. 7, II, mm. 1–4

3. Identify, with exact RNs, the tonicizations in the following spots of example 18.2:

   a) Measure 2 (to the fermata).

   b) Measure 3, beats 1–2.

   c) Measures 5–6.

   d) Measure 8 (to the fermata).

The phrase in m. 8, beat 4 to m. 10, beat 1, constitutes a secondary key area. What degree is tonicized? Analyze this phrase with RNs using secondary key area notation.

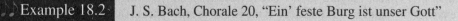

Example 18.2   J. S. Bach, Chorale 20, "Ein' feste Burg ist unser Gott"

4. Refer to anthology, no. 5 (Vivaldi, Concerto in GM, op. 3, no. 3). Analyze and provide RNs for the following tonicizations:

   a) Measures 7–10.

   b) Measures 11–15 (analyze these measures as a secondary key area).

   c) Measures 17–18.

   d) Measures 19–20.

   e) Measures 26–27.

5. Analyze example 18.3. What progression is it based on? What kind of chords is this progression built on? Can you comment on some special voice-leading properties we studied in this chapter?

Example 18.3   W. A. Mozart, Symphony no. 41 in CM, *Jupiter*, K. 551, II, mm. 58–61

6. Analyze example 18.4. The key of this passage is AM.

   a) Mm. 31–38 are based on a sequential pattern. Analyze the passage with RNs, and identify the exact type of harmonic sequence.

   b) Mm. 39–45 are based on a different sequential pattern than the previous one. Identify the exact type of harmonic sequence.

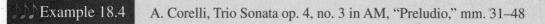

♪♪♪ Example 18.4   A. Corelli, Trio Sonata op. 4, no. 3 in AM, "Preludio," mm. 31–48

KEYBOARD HARMONY

1. Play and learn the progressions in example 18.13 of the textbook. Listen to the role of secondary dominants in these elaborations of the I–V–I progression.

2. Play the keyboard progressions in example 18.5 in CM, GM, DM, FM, B♭M; and Cm, Em, Dm, Bm, and Gm, where minor mode applies. Listen to the secondary dominants and to the chromatic voice leading as you play.

Example 18.5

3. Soprano-bass patterns. Refer to examples 18.11 and 18.12 in the textbook. Play the soprano-bass patterns in that example at the piano, adding inner voices in keyboard texture in the same major and minor keys suggested in exercise 2.

4. Sequences. Play and learn all the sequences in the following textbook examples: 18.15a, b, and f, 18.17, and 18.19, in CM, GM, and FM, and in Cm, Gm, and Fm. As an additional exercise, realize the sequences in textbook, worksheet 18, exercise 5; and workbook, chapter 18, exercise 6.

5. Roman-numeral realization. To practice realization of Roman-numeral progressions, realize the following exercises at the piano, using keyboard texture: textbook, worksheet 18, exercises 2 and 3a; and workbook, chapter 18, exercises 2a and 3.

6. Figured-bass realization. To practice realization of figured-bass progressions, realize the following exercises at the piano, using keyboard texture: textbook, worksheet 18, exercise 3b; and workbook, chapter 18, exercise 2b.

7. Melody harmonization. To practice melody harmonization, realize the following exercises at the piano, using keyboard texture: textbook, worksheet 18, exercise 4; and workbook, chapter 18, exercises 4 and 5.

Chapter 19

Secondary Leading-Tone Chords

EXERCISE 1   Analysis.

1. Identify with RNs (Roman numerals) all the _ _ _ _ rations and secondary functions in the following examples.

   a) Example 19.1.
   b) Example 19.2.
   c) Refer back to example 17.1 (Bach, Chorale 107). Identify _ _ _ tonicizations in the second phrase (mm. 17–18) that use secondary diminished seventh chords. Provide _ _ _ _ RNs.

2. a) Provide a RN analysis of example 19.3. Write the RNs in the spa_ _ _ _ _ _luded under the chords.

   b) Identify on the score all the circled NCTs (nonchord tones). Provide _ _ _ _ 's (such as 4–3, 9–8) for suspensions where needed.

Example 19.1   G. Verdi, *Il trovatore,* act II, no. 15, mm. 13–17

EXERCISE 2   Write and resolve the following secondary diminished seventh chords. The resolution should be to the appropriate tonicized chord, in root position or inversion as required by the voice leading in the bass.

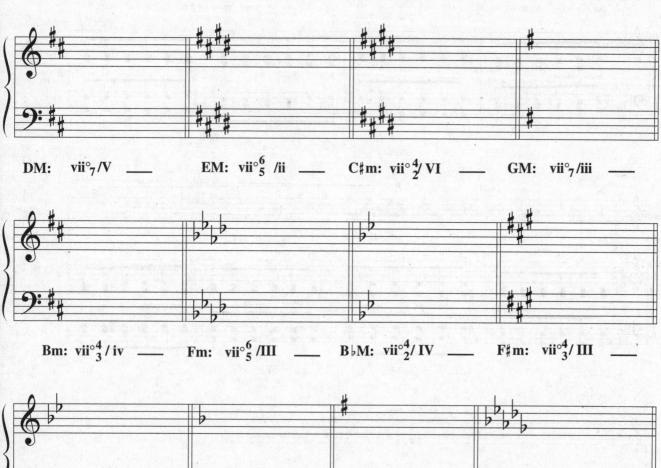

DM: vii°$_7$/V ____   EM: vii°$^6_5$/ii ____   C♯m: vii°$^4_2$/VI ____   GM: vii°$_7$/iii ____

Bm: vii°$^4_3$/iv ____   Fm: vii°$^6_5$/III ____   B♭M: vii°$^4_2$/IV ____   F♯m: vii°$^4_3$/III ____

Gm: vii°$^6_5$/iv ____   FM: vii°$_7$/IV ____   Em: vii°$^4_2$/V ____   D♭M: vii°$^4_3$/vi ____

EXERCISE 3   Realize the following short progressions in four voices.

GM: I   vii°$^4_3$/ V   V$_6$ I   FM: I   ii$^6_5$ vii°$_7$/V   V   I   EM: I   vii°$^6_5$/   i   V   I

EXERCISE 4   Realize the following figured bass in four voices. Provide a RN analysis.

EXERCISE 5

1. Write progressions (bass and RNs) using the chords required in each case. Make sure you resolve the required chords correctly.

   a) vii°$^4_3$/V, vii°$^6_5$/iv, vii°$_7$/V.

   b) vii°$_7$/ii, vii°$^6_5$/vi, vii°$^6_5$/V.

a.

F♯m:

b.

B♭M:

2. Choose one of your own progressions from exercise 5, and use it as a harmonic basis to compose a phrase for a melodic instrument and keyboard accompaniment.

EXERCISE 6

1. Harmonize the following melody with a bass and RNs. If possible, follow the suggested harmonic rhythm. Harmonize the notes marked with an asterisk with a secondary diminished seventh chord. Include a secondary key area of III where required by the melody.

2. When you are sure that your harmonization is correct, copy the melody again on your own music paper and, below it, provide a left-hand keyboard realization of your harmonization.

Britain

KEYBOARD HARMONY

1. Play and learn the progressions in example 19.13 of the textbook. Listen to the role of secondary leading-tone chords in these elaborations of the I–V–I progression.

2. Play the keyboard progressions in example 19.4 in a variety of keys. (Suggested keys: CM, DM, AM, E♭M, A♭M, and their relative minors.)

♪♪♪ Example 19.4

3. Roman-numeral realization. To practice realization of Roman-numeral progressions, realize the following exercises at the piano, using keyboard texture: textbook, worksheet 19, exercises 3c and d, and 5; and workbook, chapter 19, exercises 2 and 3.

4. Figured-bass realization. To practice realization of figured-bass progressions, realize the following exercise at the piano, using keyboard texture: textbook, worksheet 19, exercises 3a and b, and 4; and workbook, chapter 19, exercise 4.

5. Melody harmonization. To practice melody harmonization, realize the following exercises at the piano, using keyboard texture: textbook, worksheet 19, exercise 6; and workbook, chapter 19, exercise 6.

Chapter 20

Modulation to Closely Related Keys

EXERCISE 1 Analysis. Study and analyze the following modulations, and complete the following steps for each of them.

1. Identify (and write in the space below) the keys involved in the modulation.

2. Identify (and write in the space below) the modulation procedure from among the following:
   a) Diatonic pivot chord.
   b) Chromatic pivot chord.
   c) Chromatic modulation.
   d) Phrase modulation.
   e) Abrupt modulation.
   f) Sequential modulation or tonicizations.

3. If it is a pivot chord modulation, identify the exact pivot or pivots, and label it or them on the score with the pivot chord bracket notation, indicating the function of the chord in both keys.

4. For a chromatic modulation, circle the exact passage where chromatic voice leading is used to modulate.

5. For phrase, abrupt, or sequential modulations, mark the exact spot or spots where modulation occurs.

Examples for Analysis

1. Anthology, no. 12, Bach, French Suite no. 5, Gavotte, mm. 1–8.

2. Example 20.1.

Example 20.1   A. Beach, "Elle et moi," mm. 13–23

3. Anthology, no. 12, Bach, French Suite no. 5, Gavotte, mm. 9–16.

4. Example 20.2.

Example 20.2   W. A. Mozart, Piano Sonata in CM, K. 330, II, mm. 21–28

5. Example 20.3.

Example 20.3   R. Schumann, "Nachtlied," op. 96, no. 1, mm. 7–14

6. Example 20.4.

Example 20.4   R. Schumann, "Der Dichter spricht," from *Scenes from Childhood,* op. 15, mm. 1–8

7. Example 20.5.

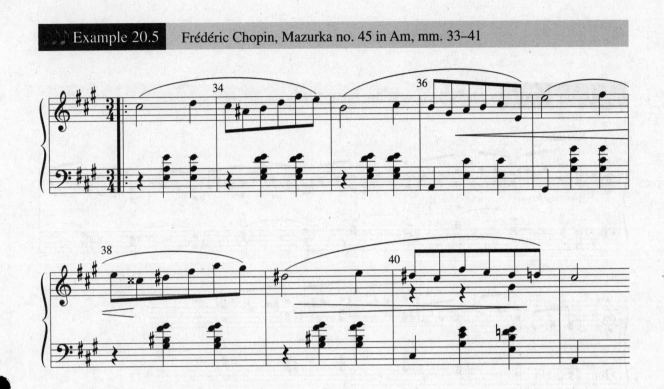

Example 20.5   Frédéric Chopin, Mazurka no. 45 in Am, mm. 33–41

8. Example 20.6.

Example 20.6   Maria Szymanowska, Etude in Dm, mm. 1–9

EXERCISE 2   The following statements refer to diatonic pivot chord relationships. Fill in the blank in each statement.

1. ii in _____ becomes iv in Am.

2. _____ in AM becomes vi in DM.

3. vi in FM becomes ii in _____.

4. ii° in Bm becomes _____ in DM.

EXERCISE 3   The following two progressions represent modulations by diatonic pivot chord.

Progression a. Provide RNs (Roman numerals) for the given bass, accounting for the modulation and indicating the pivot chord with the usual bracket. Use secondary dominants or diminished seventh chords where possible.

a.

Progression b. Write a bass line for the given RNs. Be careful to modulate to the right key.

b.

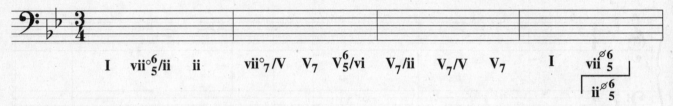

I $vii°{}^6_5/ii$ ii $vii°_7/V$ V_7 $V{}^6_5/vi$ V_7/ii V_7/V V_7 I $vii{}^{ø6}_5$
$ii{}^{ø6}_5$

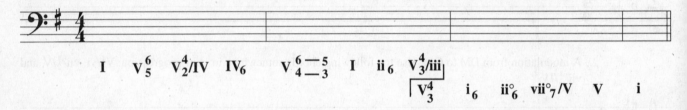

$V{}^6_4 — {}^5_3$ i $V{}^6_5$ $V{}^4_2/iv$ iv_6 $vii°{}^6_5/iv$ iv $vii°{}^4_2$ $V{}^6_4 — {}^5_3$ i

EXERCISE 4   The following progression represents a chromatic modulation. Write a bass line for the given RNs.

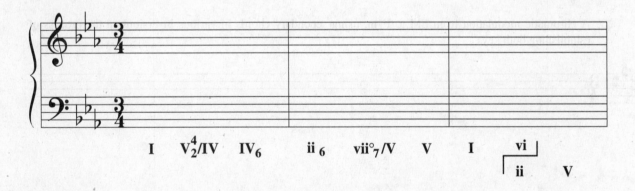

I $V{}^6_5$ $V{}^4_2/IV$ IV_6 $V{}^6_4 — {}^5_3$ I ii_6 $V{}^4_3/iii$
$V{}^4_3$ i_6 $ii°_6$ $vii°_7/V$ V i

EXERCISE 5   Realize the following progression in four voices.

I $V{}^4_2/IV$ IV_6 ii_6 $vii°_7/V$ V I vi
ii V

I $vii°_7/IV$ IV $vii°_7/V$ $V{}^6_4 — {}^5_3$ I

EXERCISE 6   After you are sure that your bass line for exercise 4 is correct, realize the progression in four voices in the space below.

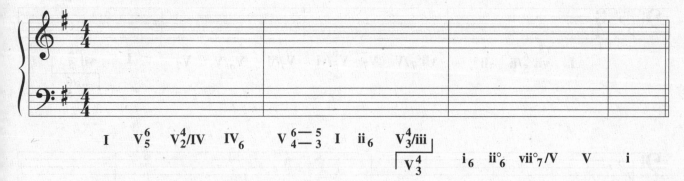

$$\text{I} \quad \text{V}^6_5 \quad \text{V}^4_2/\text{IV} \quad \text{IV}_6 \quad \text{V}^{6-5}_{4-3} \quad \text{I} \quad \text{ii}_6 \quad \text{V}^4_3/\text{iii}$$
$$\text{V}^4_3 \quad \text{i}_6 \quad \text{ii}^\circ_6 \quad \text{vii}^\circ_7/\text{V} \quad \text{V} \quad \text{i}$$

EXERCISE 7   Write the following modulations (bass and RNs). Choose an appropriate pivot chord for each of them, and indicate it with the customary bracket.

1. A modulation from Fm to A♭M. Use the following chords somewhere in your progression, along with any other chords you want: $\text{vii}^{\circ 4}_3/\text{V}$, $\text{vii}^{\circ 6}_5/\text{ii}$, and an irregular resolution of V^6_5/V.

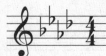

2. A modulation from DM to GM. Use the following chords somewhere in your progression: V^4_3/vi, $\text{vii}^{\circ 4}_2/\text{V}$, and $\text{vii}^{\circ 4}_3/\text{IV}$.

3. A chromatic modulation from EM to F♯m, using secondary chords in various inversions in the process of establishing both keys.

EXERCISE 8   Harmonize the following chorale ("Jesu, meine Freude") with a bass line and RNs, accounting for possible modulations. After you are sure that your harmonization works, add the two inner voices.

EXERCISE 9   Write simple keyboard accompaniments for the following modulating periods by Haydn. Provide RNs for your harmonizations and indicate your pivot chord in each case.

a.

KEYBOARD HARMONY

1. Practice the modulating keyboard progressions from example 20.7 in a variety of keys. Hear and understand the modulating process in each case (by either pivot chord or chromatic motion).

♪♪ Example 20.7

2. Roman-numeral realization. To practice realization of modulations from Roman-numeral progressions, realize the following exercises at the piano, using keyboard texture: textbook, worksheet 20, exercises 4b and 6;
   and workbook, chapter 20, exercises 3b, 4, 5 and 6.

3. Melody harmonization. To practice harmonization of modulating melodies, realize the following exercises at
   the piano, using keyboard texture: textbook, worksheet 20, exercises 8 and 9; and workbook, chapter 20, exercises 8 and 9.

Chapter 21

Small Forms: Binary and Ternary; Variation Forms

EXERCISE 1   Analysis. Analyze the following pieces. For each of them, determine and discuss the formal and tonal types, the key areas in the complete piece, and construct a bubble diagram using the given line. The diagram should show sections (labeled with letters) and tonal motion.

1. Anthology, no. 12, Bach, French Suite no. 5, Gavotte.

   a) Form and formal type:

   b) Key areas:

   c) Bubble diagram:

2. Anthology, no. 7, *Notebook for Anna Magdalena Bach,* Polonaise.

   a) Form and formal type:

   b) Key areas:

   c) Bubble diagram:

---

3. Example 21.1.

   a) Form and formal type:

   b) Key areas:

   c) Bubble diagram:

Example 21.1   L. v. Beethoven, String Quartet in B♭M, op. 18, no. 6, Trio

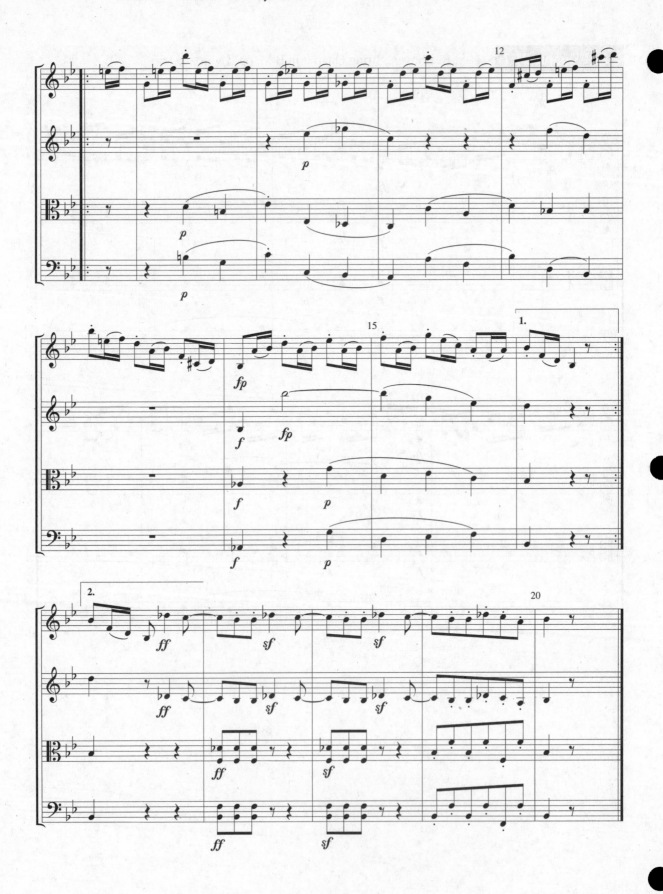

4. Anthology, no. 37, Kuhlau, Sonatina, II.

   a) Form and formal type:

   b) Key areas:

   c) Bubble diagram:

5. Example 21.2.

   a) Form and formal type:

   b) Key areas:

   c) Bubble diagram:

Example 21.2   J. S. Bach, Bourrée

6. Anthology, no. 44, Chopin, Mazurka no. 43 in Gm.

   a) Form and formal type:

   b) Key areas:

   c) Bubble diagram:

EXERCISE 2   Listen (with score) to Brahms, Symphony no. 4 in Em, op. 98, IV.

   a) What kind of variations are these (sectional or continuous)? Explain.

   b) Considering that mm. 1–8 are the theme and mm. 253–end is a finale, and hence either not counting as a variation, how many variations are there?

   c) What is the overall form of the movement? Provide a diagram.

   d) A new section begins in m. 97, and it lasts until m. _____. Which musical parameter(s) set(s) this section apart from the previous one?

   The variations in this section are numbers _____ through _____.

   e) Are there any variations in the major mode? Provide measure numbers and variation numbers.

   f) What is the formal function of mm. 81–96?

   g) Is there a return (other than the finale at m. 253)? Where?

h) What instruments(s) carry the main melody (theme) in mm. 1–8?

And in mm. 49–56?

i) If we call mm. 57–65 a figural variation, notate the rhythm of the most characteristic motive/figure. (Listen for it!)

j) Measures 153–161 are an ornamental variation. What instrument carries the notes of the main theme, but now altered by the addition of other notes?

EXERCISE 3   Analytical paper. Choose one of the pieces you just studied in exercise 1, and write a brief analytical paper on it. With good narrative prose, discuss form, formal and tonal types, sections, key areas and tonal motion, and thematic/motivic relationships. Identify also special compositional techniques (such as imitation, sequence, textural inversion between hands), and discuss the techniques of motivic and thematic development used in the piece. Attach (and comment on) a bubble diagram. You may use the various analytical discussions of pieces you have found in this chapter's text as possible models for your paper (and your narrative).

EXERCISE 4   Harmonize the following chorale ("Von Gott will ich nicht lassen") with a bass line and RNs (Roman numerals), accounting for possible modulations. As an additional exercise, you can also fill in inner voices.

EXERCISE 5 Harmonize the following two folk melodies and write realizations of your harmonizations in keyboard style.

EXERCISE 6   Write a keyboard accompaniment for the following melody and provide RNs for your harmonization. What formal and tonal types does this melody represent?

EXERCISE 7   Compose two modulating periods (melody and accompaniment in keyboard style) based on the given motives. The modulating periods by Haydn in the worksheet and workbook for chapter 20 may serve as models. You may compose the melody first and then write the accompaniment, or write both at the same time.

1. Modulate to the key of V. A possibility is to write an antecedent in CM, ending on a HC, and a parallel consequent that modulates to V (as in Mozart's familiar "Tema" from his DM sonata). Remember that the easiest way to modulate to V is to introduce ♯4̂, as in the example provided below.

a. **Example**

2. Modulate to the relative major key (III). Remember: to modulate to III, cancel the leading-tone accidental in minor and resolve either the new leading tone or the new $\hat{5}$ to the new $\hat{1}$. We do not need any new accidentals in this modulation (see the example provided below).

b.   **Example**

Chapter 22

Contrapuntal Genres

EXERCISE 1   Write a brief analytical paper on Bach's Invention no. 4 in Dm (score and recording available at the library). You may use the discussion of Invention no. 3 in DM in chapter 22 of the textbook as a model. The organization by sections used in that analysis is perfectly appropriate for your paper. Make sure you discuss the following aspects of the Dm invention:

1. Sections and their function (exposition, episodes, return, codetta). Cadences and key areas. Any pedals? What is their harmonic and formal function?

2. How are all the keys in the piece related among themselves?

3. Thematic content: What are the musical characteristics of the subject? Is the subject always present? Does it appear in any varied forms (such as inverted, or elaborated in any way)?

4. What developmental techniques are used and where (circle of fifths, sequence, fragmentation, etc.)? What is the role of imitation in the piece? Are there sections of "give-and-take" texture?

EXERCISE 2   Analyze Mozart's String Quartet, K. 173, IV (Fugue). Answer the following questions, and turn in an annotated copy of the score (which you will find at your music library).

1. Exposition:
   a) How long is the subject?

   b) Is the answer real or tonal?

   c) Is there a countersubject? If yes, where?

   d) Is there a bridge? Where?

   e) What are its specific formal and tonal functions?

   f) The exposition ends with the first full authentic cadence in the piece. Where, and in what key?

2. Middle sections:
   a) Episode 1 (mm. numbers):   Its tonal function is:
   b) Middle entry group 1: It begins in m.   in the key of
                            It ends in m.   in the key of
   c) Episode 2 (mm. numbers):   Its tonal function is:
   d) The entry in m. 28 is in the key of:
   e) Episode 3 (mm. 31–35) leads to a series of entries in mm. 35–44. Mark all of them on the score. What happened to the subject in these entries?

   What is the effect of whatever happened to the subject from a metric point of view?

   What name does this type of section have in a fugue?

   f) Mark on the score the entries in mm. 45–51. What is the key?
   g) Measures 52–61: Mark the entries. Again, what happens to the subject? What kind of section is this?
      Measures 58–61: What kind of texture is this?

         Why? Where does it lead?

         What is the chord in m. 61?

         Why does it have a fermata?

3. Closing sections:
   a) What is the key of mm. 62-end?
   b) What is the formal/tonal function of the section beginning in m. 62?

   c) Considering the metric relationship among entries in this section (mm. 62–69), what is this section?

   d) How are the viola and second violin subjects related to the cello and first violin in these measures?

   e) Measures 70–73: What is this section? How are the entries related (metrically) to those in the previous section?

   f) Is there a pedal in the closing section? If yes, on what scale degree?

EXERCISE 3   On your own music paper, write four fugal subjects in different meters and keys. Determine whether the answer to each of your subjects should be real or tonal. Then, write the appropriate answer for each of them.

EXERCISE 4   Harmonize the following melody with a left-hand keyboard figuration, using borrow   hord
where possible. Be sure to check your outer-voice frame for correct voice leading.

FM:

EXERCISE 5   Write a nonmodulating period using the given motive, and provide a keyboard harmon
Use several instances of mixture (borrowed chords, change of mode) in your harmonization.

8 measures

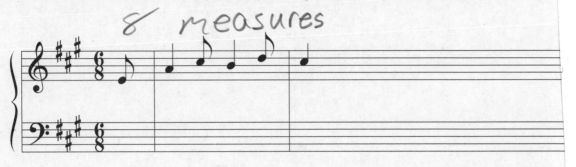

KEYBOARD HARMONY

1. Practice the keyboard progressions from example 23.6 in a variety of keys. Because these progressions use chords from the minor mode borrowed in the major mode, they should be played *only in major keys*.

Example 23.6

2. Soprano-bass patterns. Refer to example 23.15 in the textbook. Play the soprano-bass patterns in that example at the piano, adding inner voices in keyboard texture in the same major keys you used in exercise 1.

3. Roman-numeral realization. To practice realization of Roman-numeral progressions, realize the following exercises at the piano, using keyboard texture: textbook, worksheet 23, exercises 3a and c; and workbook, chapter 23, exercise 3.

4. Figured-bass realization. To practice realization of figured-bass progressions, realize the following exercises at the piano, using keyboard texture: textbook, worksheet 23, exercises 3b and 4; and workbook, chapter 23, exercise 2.

5. Melody harmonization. To practice melody harmonization, realize the following exercises at the piano, using keyboard texture: textbook, worksheet 23, exercise 5; and workbook, chapter 23, exercise 4.

KEYBOARD HARMONY

1. Practice the keyboard progression from example 24.3 in a variety of M and m keys. Hear the sound and resolution of the ♭II₆ chords in the progression.

♪♪♪ Example 24.3

CM: I   ♭II₆   V   I   ♭II₆   vii°₇/V   V$^6_4$ – $^7_5_3$ I

2. Roman-numeral and figured-bass realization. To practice realization of Roman-numeral and figured-bass progressions, realize the following exercises at the piano, using keyboard texture: textbook, worksheet 24, exercises 3 and 4; and workbook, chapter 24, exercises 2 and 3.

3. Melody harmonization. To practice melody harmonization, realize the following exercises at the piano, using keyboard texture: textbook, worksheet 24, exercise 5; and workbook, chapter 24, exercise 4.

Chapter 25

Augmented Sixth Chords

EXERCISE 1   Analysis. Identify the +6 chords in each of the following examples.

1. Identify the type of +6 chord ("nationality"). If it is a Gr +6, is it spelled with a ♭$\hat{3}$ or a ♯$\hat{2}$?

2. Provide RNs for the actual +6 chord and also for the chords that precede and follow it.

3. Does the +6 chord resolve directly to V? Does it resolve to V through some other harmonies?

Are parallel 5ths avoided?

Examples for Analysis:

1. Example 25.1.

♩♩♩ Example 25.1   W. A. Mozart, Symphony no. 39 in E♭M, K. 543, IV, mm. 130–137

2. Example 25.2.

Example 25.2   J. Haydn, String Quartet in DM, op. 64, no. 5, I, mm. 46–50

3. Example 25.3.

Example 25.3   Gioachino Rossini, *Petite messe solennelle*, Credo, mm. 14–18

4. Example 25.4a.

Example 25.4b.

Example 25.4   L. v. Beethoven, String Quartet in Cm, op. 18, no.4, IV, mm. 5–8 and 147–153

5. Example 25.5.

Example 25.5   L. v. Beethoven, Piano Sonata in E♭M, op. 7, II, mm. 72–74

6. Example 25.6.

Example 25.6   W. A. Mozart, Symphony no. 40 in Gm, K. 550, I, mm. 12–16

EXERCISE 2   Realize the following short progressions in four voices. Add RNs to the progressions with a figured bass.

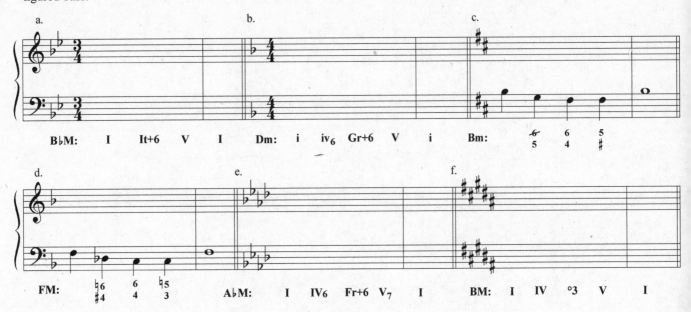

EXERCISE 3   Realize the following progression in four voices. Provide a RN analysis.

EXERCISE 4   Harmonize the following melody with a keyboard accompaniment. Include an +6 chord where appropriate.

EXERCISE 2. Realize the following short progressions in four-voice, and add V_5^6 to the progressions with a figured bass.

EXERCISE 3. Realize the following bass and/or melody for keyboard. Perform it, too.

EXERCISE 4. Harmonize the following melody with a keyboard accompaniment. Include an augmented sixth chord at the cadence.

KEYBOARD HARMONY

1. Practice the keyboard progression from example 25.7 in a variety of M and m keys. Hear the sound and resolution of the +6 chords in the progressions. Notice especially (and enjoy!) the interesting harmonization of the descending chromatic bass, which you can now realize with chords you have studied (example 25.7c).

Example 25.7

2. Roman-numeral and figured-bass realization. To practice realization of Roman-numeral and figured-bass progressions, realize the following exercises at the piano, using keyboard texture: textbook, worksheet 25, exercises 3 and 4; and workbook, chapter 25, exercises 2 and 3.

3. Melody harmonization. To practice melody harmonization, realize the following exercises at the piano, using keyboard texture: textbook, worksheet 25, exercise 5; and workbook, chapter 25, exercise 4.

Chapter 26

Chromatic Modulatory Techniques: Modulation to Distantly Related Keys I

EXERCISE 1   Analysis.

1. The following modulation features a chromatic pivot chord. Analyze the complete passage with RNs (Roman numerals), and explain the modulation and the pivot chord.

♪♪ Example 26.1   L. v. Beethoven, Six Variations, op. 76, Var. VI, mm. 27–38

2. The following examples feature the ♭II key area and/or modulations by enharmonic reinterpretation of +6. Analyze each of them, identify the modulations or the ♭II key area, the keys involved, and the exact function of the pivot chord in each of the keys.

a) Example 26.2.

Example 26.2   F. Schubert, Piano Sonata in Am, op. 164, I, mm. 57–67

b) Anthology, no. 51, Liszt, *Consolation*, no. 4. The phrase in mm. 16–18 is in DM. A sudden phrase modulation takes place in m. 18. To what key? How does the chord in m. 18, beats 1–2, function in each of the keys?

c) Example 26.3.

1) The main key of the passage is FM. What secondary key area of FM is featured?

2) Explain the return to FM in mm. 47–53.

Example 26.3   F. Schubert, Piano Sonata in Am, op. 164, I, mm. 41–53

3. The passage by Schubert in example 26.4 begins in B♭m.

   a) What is the chord in mm. 139–140, and to what chord does it resolve?

   b) What is the key area in mm. 152–159?

   c) The modulation to this second key area takes place in mm. 146–152. Explain how this modulation works.

d) What is the key in mm. 162–167?

e) What is the chord in mm. 160–161, and how does it function in AM? Have we seen this same sonority elsewhere in this passage in a different key and with a different function?

f) The modulation in mm. 157–162 is to a closely related key by means of a diatonic pivot chord. Explain.

g) Comment on the compositional/contrapuntal techniques used in this passage, especially in mm. 142–166.

Example 26.4   F. Schubert, Sonata for Violin and Piano, op. posth. 162, IV, mm. 133–167

4. The following examples feature modulation by enharmonic reinterpretation of vii°₇ chords. Analyze each of them, identify the modulations, the keys involved, and the exact function of the pivot chord in each of the keys.

a) Example 26.5.

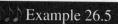 **Example 26.5**   L. v. Beethoven, Piano Sonata in Cm, op. 13, *Pathétique*, I, mm. 133–136

b) Example 26.6. This passage begins in AM.
   1) What key area is featured in mm. 141–144?
   2) What is the function of the first chord in m. 140 in each of the keys?

   3) The same chord is featured again in m. 145, leading back to AM. What is its function here?

Example 26.6   L. v. Beethoven, Piano Sonata in AM, op. 2 no. 2, IV, mm. 138–148

EXERCISE 2   Write the following chromatic pivot chord modulations (bass and RNs, with indication of the pivot chord).

1. From FM to AM using ♭II₆ of AM as a pivot.

FM:

2. From AM to BM using a secondary dominant in AM as pivot.

AM:

3. From B♭M to CM using a vii°₇ chord with a secondary function in both keys.

B♭M:

EXERCISE 3   The following RNs represent modulations by enharmonic reinterpretation of the Gr +6 chord. Write the bass line for each progression, and indicate what key we have modulated to in each case.

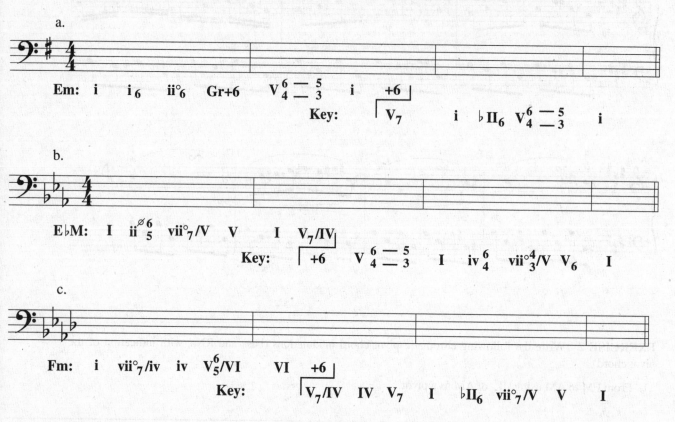

a.

Em: i   i$_6$ ii°$_6$ Gr+6   V$_4^6$ — $_3^5$ i   +6

Key: V$_7$ i   ♭II$_6$ V$_4^6$ — $_3^5$ i

b.

E♭M: I   ii$_5^{ø6}$ vii°$_7$/V   V   I   V$_7$/IV

Key: +6   V$_4^6$ — $_3^5$ I   iv$_4^6$ vii°$_3^{4}$/V   V$_6$ I

c.

Fm: i   vii°$_7$/iv   iv   V$_5^6$/VI   VI   +6

Key: V$_7$/IV   IV   V$_7$ I   ♭II$_6$ vii°$_7$/V   V   I

EXERCISE 4   Write the following modulating progression in four voices. Provide both enharmonic spellings for the pivot chord. Write the key signature for the new key after the double bar (in the space marked with an asterisk).

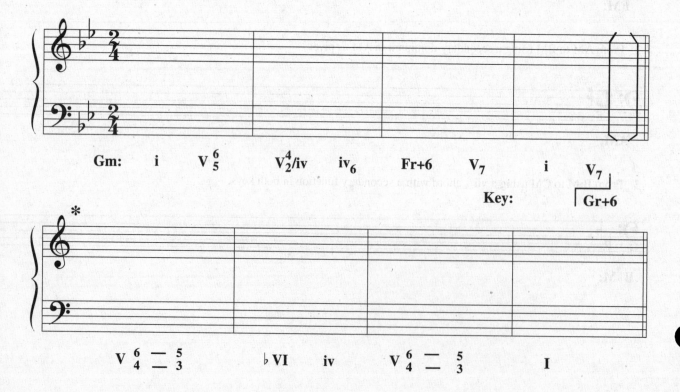

Gm: i   V$_5^6$ V$_2^4$/iv   iv$_6$ Fr+6   V$_7$ i   V$_7$

Key: Gr+6

*

V$_4^6$ — $_3^5$ ♭VI   iv   V$_4^6$ — $_3^5$ I

EXERCISE 5

1. Write and resolve vii°₇ in E♭M in exercise 5a. This chord may be used to modulate to three other major keys by respelling it enharmonically. Indicate the keys and provide the spelling (leaving the chord in the same position), the correct RN, and the correct resolution to the corresponding tonic in each of the new keys. For a reference of what you are doing exactly, see example 26.15b in the textbook (although in that example the chords are not resolved).

2. In exercise 5b follow the same process as in 5a, but now show how vii°₇ in Gm functions in three other minor keys.

a.   b.

key 1: E♭M   key 2:   key 3:   key 4:   key 1: Gm   key 2:   key 3:   key 4:

3. The following statements refer to enharmonically respelled vii°₇ chords. Fill in the blank in each statement.

  a) vii°₇ in A♭ becomes _____ in D.
  b) _____ in E becomes vii°₂⁴ in B♭.
  c) vii°₃⁴ in _____ becomes vii°₇ in A.
  d) vii°₂⁴ in F becomes vii°₇ in _____.

EXERCISE 6   The following RNs represent a modulation by enharmonic reinterpretation of vii°₇. Write the bass line, and indicate what key we have modulated to.

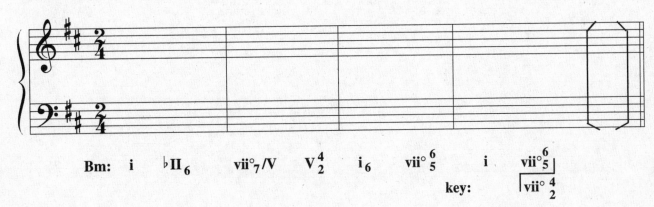

EXERCISE 7   Write the following modulating progression in four voices. Provide both enharmonic spellings for the pivot chord. Write the key signature for the new key after the double bar (in the space marked with an asterisk).

V $\frac{6}{4}$ — $\frac{7}{5}$ ... I   V $\frac{6}{5}$ vii° $\frac{4}{2}$/ii   ii $\frac{6}{4}$ Fr+6   V   I

EXERCISE 8 Write your own modulating progressions (bass and RNs) using Gr +6 and vii°$_7$ chords as pivots.

1. A modulation from Fm to Em using an enharmonic reinterpretation of the Gr +6.

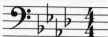

Fm:

2. A modulation from AM to Cm using an enharmonic reinterpretation of vii°$_5^6$ in AM.

AM:

KEYBOARD HARMONY

1. Practice the keyboard progressions from example 26.7 in a variety of keys. Hear and understand the modulating process in each case (by either chromatic pivot chord or enharmonic reinterpretation). If you are sufficiently proficient at the keyboard, practice improvising some similar progressions, especially using +6 and vii°₇ chords to modulate to distant keys.

Example 26.7

♪♪♪ Example 26.7 **Continued**

2. To practice playing modulations by enharmonic reinterpretation of the Gr +6 from Roman numerals, realize the following exercises at the piano, using keyboard texture: textbook, worksheet 26, exercises 5 and 6; and workbook, chapter 26, exercises 3 and 4.

3. To practice playing modulations by enharmonic reinterpretation of vii°₇ from Roman numerals, realize the following exercises at the piano, using keyboard texture: textbook, worksheet 26, exercises 8 and 9; and workbook, chapter 26, exercises 6 and 7.

Chapter 27

Modulation to Distantly Related Keys II; Linear Chromaticism I

EXERCISE 1   Analysis.

1. Study the chordal relationships in the following passage, and explain with the correct terms how the chords are related.

> **♪ Example 27.1**   G. Verdi, *Otello*, act I, scene III, mm. 46–50

2. Study the following modulations. For each of them, determine the following points:
   a) What keys are involved?
   b) How are the keys related (diatonic third, chromatic third, half step, etc.)
   c) What is the RN relationship between the keys? (Be aware of possible enharmonic spellings of keys.)
   d) What type of modulation is it?
   e) If it is a common tone (CT) modulation, what is the CT? Or is there, perhaps, more than one CT?
   f) What are the functions of the triads used in the CT modulation?

Examples for Analysis

1. Example 27.2.

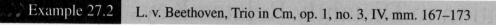

Example 27.2   L. v. Beethoven, Trio in Cm, op. 1, no. 3, IV, mm. 167–173

2. Example 27.3.

   a) First, study the modulation in mm. 9–12.

   b) Then analyze the return to the original key in mm. 12–16.

Example 27.3   F. Schubert, Waltz in A♭M, op. 9 no. 2

3. The following passages include examples of altered triads, Fr +6 as an altered dominant, embellishing +6, or CT°7 chords. Identify and label the particular chord illustrated in each example, and determine its exact linear function (passing, neighbor/embellishing, etc.).

   a) Example 27.4.

Example 27.4   R. Schumann, "Ich kann's nicht fassen," from *Frauenliebe und Leben*, mm. 17–23

   b) Example 27.5.

Example 27.5   J. Brahms, Symphony no. 4 in Em, op. 98, IV, mm. 1–8

c) Example 27.6.

   1) Several of this chapter's chords are present in this fragment. One of them actually appears in three different keys. Another one is featured at the cadence. Identify and label all of them.

   2) What are the three keys featured in this example? How are they related?

Example 27.6   Jean Sibelius, *Finlandia*, op. 26, mm. 1–23

d) Example 27.7.

Example 27.7   F. Schubert, "Moment Musical," op. 94, no. 6, mm. 29–36

EXERCISE 2

1. List the six triads (or keys) related by chromatic third to each of the following triads (or keys). Write down both the triad name and the RN that indicates its relationship with the original triad.

2. Then, circle the four triads that have a CT with the original triad.

FM:

BM:

Gm:

C#m:

EXERCISE 3
Write a CT modulation in four voices, from Fm to a key of your choice, related with Fm by chromatic third. Include a secondary dominant and a Fr +6 in the first key area (Fm), and a tonicized ♭II chord in the second key area.

Fm:

EXERCISE 4 Realize the following short progressions in four voices. Pay attention to the RN quality (upper-case or lowercase), which may denote a chromatic third relationship (for instance, I–III is not the same, of course, as I–iii).

a.

FM: I   VI   V⁺   I

b.

Bm: i   Gr+6   V⁺   i

c.

F♯m: i   V⁺   V⁺⁴₂   i₆   ii∅₇   V°⁴₃   i

d.

EM: I   ♭III   V°⁴₃   I

e.

B♭M: I   emb+6   I   III   I

f.

AM: I   ♭II₆   vii°₇/V   V⁺   I   CT°7   I

EXERCISE 5   Write a common-tone modulation from E♭M to ♭VI, in four voices. Spell the ♭VI key enharmonically. Include an embellishing +6 and a ♭II₆ in the E♭M area, and a CT°7 and a cadential V °⁴₃ in the ♭VI area.

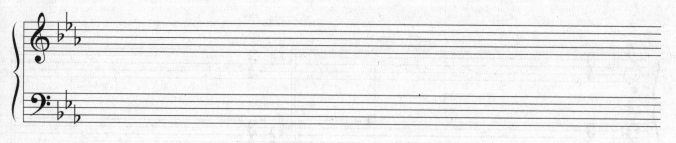

E♭M:

KEYBOARD HARMONY

1. Practice the keyboard progressions in example 27.8 in a variety of keys. Hear and understand the CT modulations to chromatic third-related keys. And pay attention to the voice leading for the linear chromatic chords included in these progressions.

Example 27.8

2. Roman-numeral realization. To practice realization of Roman-numeral progressions, realize the following exercises at the piano, using keyboard texture: textbook, worksheet 27, exercises 5 and 6; and workbook, chapter 27, exercise 4.

Chapter 28

Introduction to Large Forms

EXERCISE 1   Write a short analytical paper on Brahms's Sonata no. 2 for Violin and Piano, op. 100, I, in sonata form. The score and a recording will be available at your music library. The score can also be found in the Arlin anthology *(Music Sources).* You can use the analysis of Mozart's CM sonata in chapter 28 of the textbook, as well as the guided analysis of Beethoven's *Waldstein* sonata in the same chapter, as models for the organization of your paper. Turn in an annotated copy of the score.

   The following are some specific questions about this particular movement by Brahms that you should address in your paper.

1. How is the P area structured? Is there a single P theme?

2. How many different S themes are there? Is there a C theme?

3. What marks the end of the exposition and the beginning of the development?

4. What are the themes on which Brahms bases the development?

5. Comment on the use of (at least) the following techniques in the development: hemiola, canonic imitation, thematic inversion, diminution, fragmentation, and pedal.

6. Is there a retransition? Is it on the customary V harmony?

7. Compare carefully the recapitulation and the exposition, and comment on what is the same and what is different.

8. The movement features a coda that functions as a second development. Explain where it begins and ends, and its thematic and tonal contents.

9. While in the exposition the P theme is stated first by the piano, and then by the violin, the equivalent statement of P in the recapitulation combines the instruments in a different way. (How?) Does the statement of the beginning of P by the violin (which is missing at the beginning of the recapitulation) come later in the movement?

10. Provide a complete analysis of key areas and tonal motion in the movement, as well as a formal diagram.

EXERCISE 2   Analyze Beethoven's String Quartet in Cm, op. 18 n. 4, IV, in rondo form. The score and the recording will be available at your music library. The score can also be found in the Arlin anthology *(Music Sources)*. Turn in an annotated copy of the score with indications of thematic/sectional content and key areas for the complete movement.

Provide a formal diagram for the complete movement and answer the following questions:

1. What type of rondo form is this?

2. What is the formal design of the refrain?

3. The cadences in mm. 8, 12, and 16 are all approached by means of the same type of chord. What is it?

4. What is the formal design of the first episode?

5. How are the keys of the refrain and first episode related?

6. Compare the textures of the refrain and the first episode. How are they contrasting? What contrapuntal techniques can you identify in the first episode?

7. How is the first return of the refrain different from the original refrain?

8. What is the formal design of the second episode? How is this episode contrasting tonally?

9. How is second return of the refrain different from the previous statements of the same material?

10. What is the formal function of mm. 111–116?

11. What is the section that begins in m. 117? Have we heard this material before, and what is different here from what we heard before?

12. Explain the formal structure of mm. 125–136. What is the function of mm. 132–136 within this passage?

13. An apparent final return of the refrain begins in m. 137. What is the character, however, of the section that begins in that measure? What key areas are touched on?

14. What is the formal function of mm. 154–162? What section do they lead to? What is the distinguishing characteristic of this new presentation of old material?

15. What is the section that begins in m. 178?

16. Comment on motivic coherence in this movement:
    a) How are the motives in mm. 1 and 9 related?

    b) How are the two violin lines in mm. 9–12 related? Do the viola and cello in the same measures display a similar relationship?

    c) Is the theme of the first episode (motive in mm. 17–18 and 25–26) related to the opening motive in any way? And what about the thematic material of the second episode (m. 75)?

Chapter 29

Expanding Functional Tonality: Extended Tertian Chords; Linear Chromaticism II

EXERCISE 1 Analysis.

1. The following passages include examples of extended tertian chords. Identify and label these chords, and verify the resolution of the dissonant chord members.

   a) Example 29.1. Explain the resolution of the extended tertian chord in this example. What kind of a linear, embellishing chord does Beethoven use to connect the dominant and the tonic harmonies?

Example 29.1   L. v. Beethoven, Six Variations, op. 76, Variation V, mm. 5–8

b) Example 29.2

Example 29.2   Pyotr Ilich Tchaikovsky, *The Sleeping Beauty,* act I, no. 1, March, mm. 1–5

c) Example 29.3

Example 29.3   Maurice Ravel, Sonatina, I, mm. 22–23

d) Example 29.4

   1) What are the two chords in m. 182?

   2) Measure 183 contains a single harmony, an Em tonic chord. How do you explain the pitches in beat 1?

Example 29.4   William Grant Still, *Pastorela,* for Violin and Piano, mm. 180–192

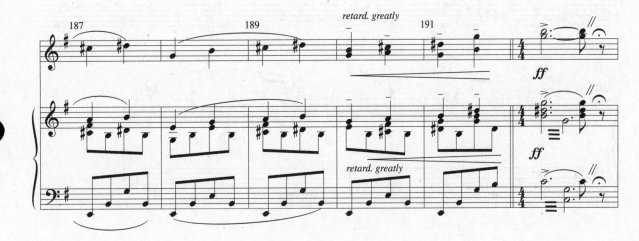

3) Think of mm. 188–192 as a modulation from Em to CM. What chord is used to modulate, and how does it function in each of the keys?

4) Provide the exact RN (Roman numeral) for the CM tonic chord in m. 192.

Example 29.5 Richard Wagner, *Tristan und Isolde,* Prelude to act III, mm. 30–43

e) Example 29.5

1) The basic harmonic content of this passage (in Fm) can be reduced to two chords. The first one is prolonged in mm. 30–37, and the second one in mm. 38–43. What are the chords?

2) These two harmonies are repeatedly embellished by means of the same two types of linear chords, which you will first find in mm. 30–31. What are they?

2. The following examples include chromatic sequences. Name the exact type of sequence, and provide the necessary figures to identify the sequential pattern.

Example 29.6   Giacomo Puccini, "Gloria," from *Messa di Gloria*, mm. 9–23

Example 29.6   Continued

a) Example 29.6

   1) Identify and analyze the chromatic sequence in this excerpt.

   2) Study the chord succession in mm. 15–17. How are these chords related (take into consideration root relationships and triadic quality)?

   3) Explain the modulation from CM to E♭M in mm. 18–20. What key relationship is this? What chord is used to modulate, and how does it function in each key?

b) Example 29.7. In this excerpt you will find two of the sequence types we have studied in this chapter.

3. Example 29.8

   a) On a separate sheet, explain the linear process in mm. 17–25 using the same concepts we applied to the analysis of Chopin's Prelude no. 4 in Em. Provide a diagram for these measures similar to the graph in example 29.20a of the textbook.

   b) What degree is tonicized in mm. 29–30?

Example 29.7   Antonio Vivaldi, "Laudamus Te," from *Gloria,* op. 103, no. 3, mm. 92–109

Example 29.8   F. Chopin, Mazurka in Am, op. 7 no. 2, mm. 17–32

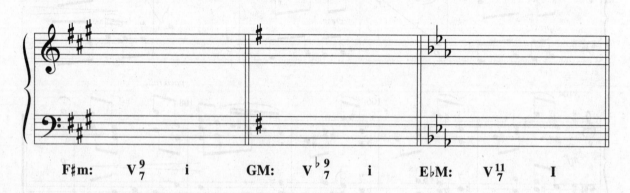

EXERCISE 2   Write and resolve the following extended tertian chords in four voices.

F#m: V$^9_7$ i   GM: V$^{\flat 9}_7$ i   E♭M: V$^{11}_7$ I

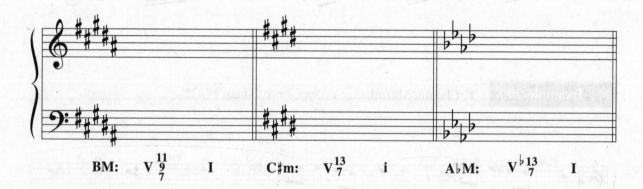

BM: V$^{11}_{\substack{9 \\ 7}}$ I   C#m: V$^{13}_7$ i   A♭M: V$^{\flat 13}_7$ I

EXERCISE 3   Realize the following progression in four voices.

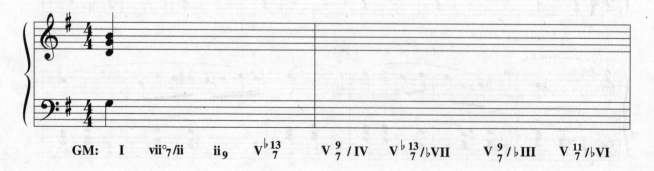

GM: I   vii°$_7$/ii   ii$_9$ V$^{\flat 13}_7$ V$^9_7$/IV   V$^{\flat 13}_7$/♭VII   V$^9_7$/♭III   V$^{11}_7$/♭VI

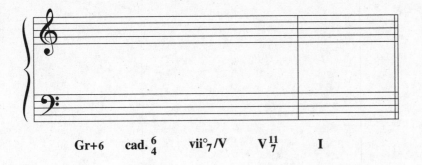

Gr+6   cad. $\frac{6}{4}$ vii°$_7$/V   V$^{11}_7$ I

EXERCISE 4   Realize the following sequential progression in four voices. Although accidentals have not been indicated in the figured bass, all $\frac{6}{5}$ chords should be inverted Mm$_7$ sonorities.

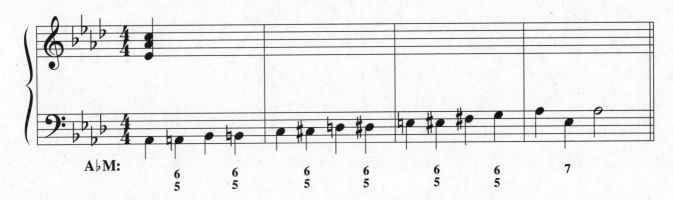

A♭M:

EXERCISE 5   Realize the following sequential progression in four voices. All necessary accidentals for this chromatic progression are indicated in the figured bass.

Gm:

EXERCISE 6   On your own music paper, compose a phrase or a period for piano using a chromatic descending 5–6 sequence.

KEYBOARD HARMONY

1. Practice the following keyboard progressions. The first two are harmonic phrases with extended tertian chords. Progression c illustrates a $\frac{7}{5} - \frac{6}{3}$ sequence, and progression d is based on Chopin's Prelude no. 4.

Example 29.9

a.

b.

c.

d.   (Chopin)

Em:

2. Practice the sequences in the following examples from the textbook: Examples 29.13a–b (two circle-of-5ths sequences), 29.14a–b (two sequences by ascending 2nds), and 29.16b–c (two descending 5–6 sequences).

3. Roman-numeral realization. To practice realization of Roman-numeral progressions, realize the following exercises at the piano, using keyboard texture: textbook, worksheet 29, exercises 2, 3, and 4; and workbook, chapter 29, exercises 2 and 3.

4. Figured-bass realization. To practice realization of sequences from figured basses, realize the following exercises at the piano, using keyboard texture: textbook, worksheet 29, exercises 5 and 6; and workbook, chapter 29, exercises 4 and 5.

Chapter 30

The German Romantic *Lied*: Chromatic Harmony in Context

EXERCISE 1   Write a short analytical paper on Schubert's song "Auf dem Flusse," from *Die Winterreise,* no. 7 (anthology, no. 42). Turn in an annotated copy of the score.

1. First, study the poem. Does the text establish two different levels of reality? What are they? How are they parallel?

2. Mark the stanzas on the music.

3. Then, analyze the tonal content of the song, with special emphasis on the following passages:

    a) Analyze mm. 7–14, indicating the pivot chord or other modulating procedures (such as common tones) between the two keys in mm. 8–9 and 12–14.

    b) The same modulation appears again in mm. 43–47. But now, in m. 47, the D♯m chord is altered to function as a chromatic pivot to a new key. Analyze this modulation carefully. How is the new key related (by RN [Roman numeral]) to the original key of Em?

    c) Explain the series of modulations in mm. 54–62.

4. Discuss the relationship between text and music in this song.

    a) How does the text in the first stanza set a duality of mood? How is it reflected in the music?

    b) What is the mood of the third and fourth stanzas, and how is it portrayed musically?

    c) The fifth stanza, on the other hand, describes a state of turbulence. This state is expressed musically in a variety of ways. Explain. What key relationship does Schubert favor in this section of emotional turbulence?

EXERCISE 2   On your own music paper, write two successive modulations using the same chords and procedures as Schubert does in mm. 41–50 of "Auf dem Flusse." That is, modulate from Em to D♯m and on to G♯m. Write this exercise in four voices, and include a RN analysis with indication of pivot chords. Attach this exercise to your paper on the Schubert song.

EXERCISE 3   Write V⁺ and resolve it to i, in Gm. This chord may be used to modulate to two other minor keys by respelling it enharmonically. Indicate the keys, and provide the spelling (leaving the chord in the same position) and the correct resolution to the tonic in each of the new keys.

Key 1: Gm   **Key 2:**   **Key 3:**

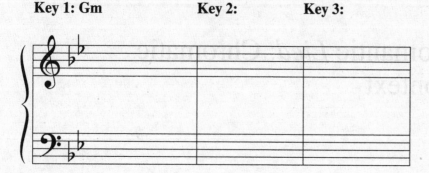

EXERCISE 4   Write a modulation in four voices by enharmonic reinterpretation of V⁺, from BM to a key of your choice.

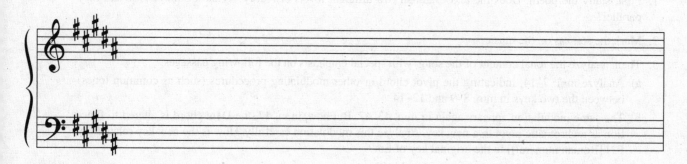

BM:

KEYBOARD HARMONY

Practice the keyboard progression from example 30.1 in a variety of keys. Hear and understand the modulations by enharmonic reinterpretation of V⁺.

Example 30.1

Chapter 31

Toward (and Beyond) the Limits of Functional Tonality

EXERCISE 1   Analysis.

1. Example 31.1.

    a) On a separate sheet, write a brief essay explaining tonal ambiguity in this example. How is F♯m implied? Is it ever established? Does the term "double-tonic complex" apply to this song? A translation of Heine's poem on which the song is based is provided. How do the tonal characteristics of this song reflect the meaning of the poem?

Example 31.1   R. Schumann, "Im wundershönen Monat Mai," from *Dichterliebe,* op. 48, mm. 14–26

♪♪ Example 31.1   Continued

"In the beautiful month of May"

In the beautiful month of May
When all the buds were bursting.
Then within my heart
Love unfolded too.

In the beautiful month of May,
When all the birds were singing,
then I confessed to her
My longing and desire.

2. Example 31.2. On a separate sheet, write a brief essay on this example, discussing the following matters:

 a) Explain the tonality of this excerpt. In what key area can mm. 1–4 best be analyzed? And mm. 5–7? How are these keys established (if they are)? Can the sonorities be analyzed functionally, linearly, or both? What are the elements of tonal ambiguity?

 b) How does melody obscure harmony in this example?

 c) Provide a harmonic reduction for the complete passage, clearly showing chordal sonorities, voice leading, and nonchord tones. Provide a RN (Roman numeral) analysis of your reduction.

 d) This symphony dates from 1896. What specific influences from Wagner and *Tristan* can you identify in this fragment?

♪♪ Example 31.2   A. Bruckner, Symphony no. 9, III, mm. 1–7

3. Comment on key area relationships in the following example.

Example 31.3   Hugo Wolf, "Die ihr schwebet," from *Spanisches Liederbuch*, mm. 1–12

es   schlum - mert mein   Kind.

4. a) Using a diagram similar to the one found in example 31.11a in the book, explain how the triads in the
following example are related by PLR transformations.

Example 31.4   F. Chopin, Ballade no. 1 in Gm, op. 23, mm. 90–95

sempre dim.

rallent.

a tempo

pp

b) The following example represents the succession of triads (key areas) in the cantabile section of Verdi's aria "Ah! sì, ben mio." Using a diagram, explain how the consonant triads in this example are related by PLR transformations.

Example 31.5   G. Verdi, "Ah! sì, ben mio," from *Il trovatore,* act III, mm. 1–22

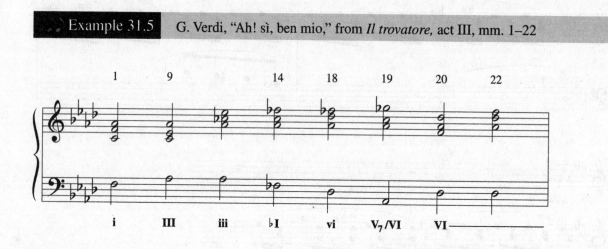

EXERCISE 2   Write two phrases for piano (melody and harmonic accompaniment) in A♭M and C♯m, respectively. Base your phrases on progressions that divide the octave symmetrically.

EXERCISE 3   Write a phrase for piano (melody and accompaniment) based on a PL parsimonious progression, beginning on an E♭M triad. (For this and the following exercises, use your own music paper.)

EXERCISE 4   Write a phrase for piano (melody and accompaniment) based on an LR parsimonious progression, beginning on a DM triad.

KEYBOARD HARMONY

1. Practice the following keyboard progressions. Progression a is modeled after Wagner's *Tristan* prelude harmony, and progressions b, c, and d are based on equal divisions of the octave.

Example 31.6

2. Practice the following PL, PR, and RL progressions directly from examples in the textbook: examples 31.11a, 31.12b, and 31.14a, respectively.

Harmony
Harmony in Context
Anthology

Anthology 1   **Tomás Luis de Victoria** (1548–1611), "Kyrie," from *Missa O magnum mysterium*

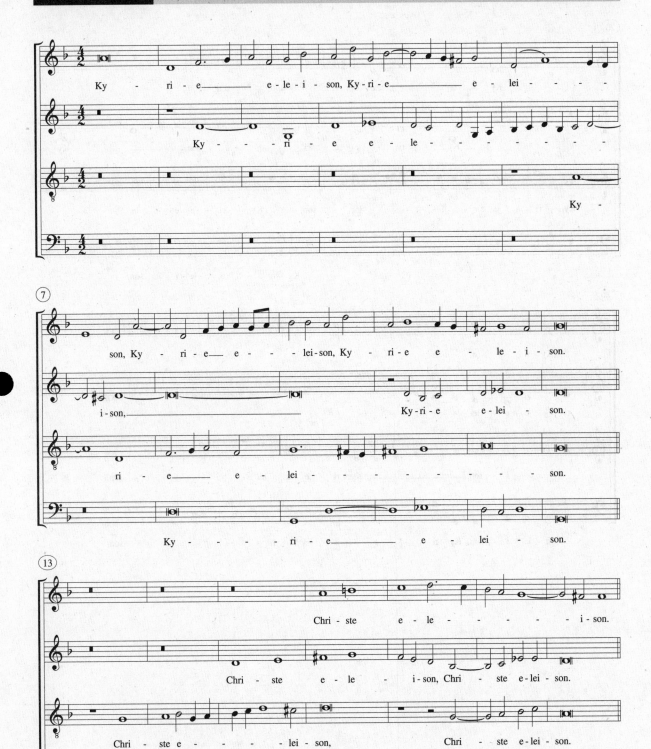

Anthology 2   Continued

Anthology 3   **Henry Purcell** (1659–1695), "Ah, Belinda," from *Dido and Aeneas*

Anthology 4   **Friedrich Wilhelm Zachau** (1663–1712), Chorale Prelude, "In dich hab ich gehoffet, Herr"

Anthology 5   **Antonio Vivaldi** (1678–1741), Concerto in GM for Violin, Strings, and Continuo from *L'estro armonico,* op. 3, no. 3, II (keyboard reduction)

Anthology 6   *Notebook for Anna Magdalena Bach* (1725), Minuet

Anthology 7   *Notebook for Anna Magdalena Bach* (1725), Polonaise

Anthology 8   **Johann Sebastian Bach** (1685–1750), Chorale 41, "Was mein Gott will, das g'scheh allzeit"

Anthology 9   **Johann Sebastian Bach** (1685–1750), Chorale 65, "Was Gott tut, das ist wohlgetan"

Anthology 10   **Johann Sebastian Bach** (1685–1750), Chorales 29, 64, and 76, "Freu' dich sehr, o meine Seele"

Anthology 11   **Johann Sebastian Bach** (1685–1750), Minuet, from French Suite no. 3 in Bm

Menuet

Anthology 12   **Johann Sebastian Bach** (1685–1750), Gavotte, from French Suite no. 5 in GM

Anthology 13   **Johann Sebastian Bach** (1685–1750), Invention no. 3 in DM

Anthology 14   **Johann Sebastian Bach** (1685–1750), *The Well–Tempered Clavier*, I, Fugue no. 2 in Cm

Anthology 14   Continued

Johann Sebastian Bach (1685–1750), *The Well–Tempered Clavier*, I,
Fugue no. 11 in FM

Anthology 15   Continued

Anthology 16   **George Frideric Handel** (1685–1759), "Lascia ch'io pianga," from *Rinaldo*

(Fine)

Aria da capo

Let me bewail
my cruel fate,
and [let me] sigh
for liberty!

Let [my] suffering break
the bonds
of my torments
through [the power] of pity.

Anthology 17   **George Frideric Handel** (1685–1759), "Amaz'd to Find the Foe So Near," from *Belshazzar*

Anthology 18   **Anna Amalie** (1723–1787), Sonata for Flute in FM, I, mm. 1–21

Joseph Haydn (1732–1809), Minuet and Trio, from Divertimento in CM, Hob. XVI:1

Menuet da capo

Anthology 20   **Joseph Haydn** (1732–1809), Piano Sonata in DM, Hob. XVI:24, II, mm. 1–24

Anthology 21   **Joseph Haydn** (1732–1809), Piano Sonata in DM, Hob. XVI:37, III

Anthology 21   Continued

♪♪ Anthology 21   Continued

Anthology 21   Continued

Anthology 22   **Joseph Boulogne, Chevalier de Saint–Georges** (1739–1799), Violin
Concerto no. 1 in GM, I, mm. 1–12

Anthology 23   **Joseph Boulogne, Chevalier de Saint–Georges** (1739–1799), Symphonie Concertante in AM, op. 10, no. 2, II, mm. 1–24

Anthology 24 **Wolfgang Amadeus Mozart** (1756–1791), Piano Sonata in DM, K. 284, Theme and Variation 7

♪♪ Anthology 25   Wolfgang Amadeus Mozart (1756–1791), Piano Sonata in CM, K. 309, I

Allegro con spirito

♪♪ Anthology 25   Continued

♪♪ Anthology 25   Continued

Anthology 25   Continued

Anthology 25   Continued

Wolfgang Amadeus Mozart (1756–1791), Piano Sonata in CM, K. 309, III, mm. 1–19

Anthology 27 **Wolfgang Amadeus Mozart** (1756–1791), Piano Sonata in AM, K. 331, I

♪♪♪ Anthology 27   Continued

♪♪ Anthology 27   Continued

♪♪♪ Anthology 27   Continued

VAR. IV

Anthology 27   Continued

Anthology 27 Continued

Anthology 28   **Wolfgang Amadeus Mozart** (1756–1791), Piano Sonata in B♭M, K. 333, III

Anthology 28   Continued

Anthology 28 Continued

♪♪ Anthology 28   Continued

♪ Anthology 28   Continued

Anthology 28   Continued

Anthology 29   **Wolfgang Amadeus Mozart** (1756–1791), "Wie Unglücklich bin ich nit," K. 147

How unhappy I am,
How languishing are my steps,
When I turn them towards you.

Only my sighs console me,
All my pains multiply
When I think of you.

♪♪ Anthology 30   Wolfgang Amadeus Mozart (1756–1791), "Die Zufriedenheit," K. 349

Mäßig

Was frag' ich viel nach Geld und Gut, wenn ich zu - frie - den

bin!   Gibt Gott mir nur ge - sun - des Blut, so hab' ich fro - hen Sinn   und

sing' aus dank - ba - rem Ge - müt mein Mor - gen und mein a - - bend - lied.

Why should I ask for money and goods
If I am happy!
If God just gives me health,
I'll have a happy mind
and sing my morning and evensong in a thankful spirit

Anthology 31   **Maria Theresia von Paradis** (1759–1824), *Sicilienne*

Anthology 32   Ludwig van Beethoven (1770–1827), Piano Sonata in Fm, op. 2, no. 1, I and III

Anthology 32   Continued

Anthology 32 Continued

Anthology 32   Continued

♪♪ Anthology 32   Continued

MENUETTO.
Allegretto.

♪♪♪ Anthology 32   Continued

Anthology 33 **Ludwig van Beethoven** (1770–1827), Piano Sonata in Cm, op. 10, no. 1, II, mm. 1–16

Anthology 34 Continued

Anthology 34   Continued

♪♪♪ Anthology 35   Continued

♪♪♪ Anthology 35   Continued

Anthology 35   Continued

Anthology 35   Continued

Anthology 35   Continued

Anthology 35 Continued

🎵🎵🎵 **Anthology 35**   Continued

Anthology 35   Continued

Anthology 35   Continued

♪♪♪ Anthology 35   **Continued**

Anthology 35   Continued

Anthology 36 **Ludwig van Beethoven** (1770–1827), Piano Sonata in E♭M, op. 7, II, mm. 15–58

Anthology 36   Continued

Anthology 37   **Friedrich Kuhlau** (1786–1832): Piano Sonatina, op. 55/4, II

Andante con espressione

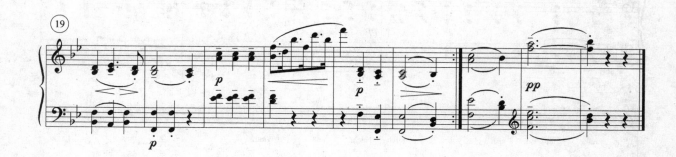

Anthology 38 Continued

21

ist der Va - ter mit sei - nem Kind; er hat den

26

Kna - - ben wohl in dem Arm, er fasst ihn sich - er, er

31

hält ihn warm.

36

Mein Sohn, was birgst du so bang dein Ge - sicht?

♪♫ Anthology 38   Continued

59

Kind,   komm,   geh   mit   mir!   gar

62

schö — — ne   Spie — — le   spiel'_____ ich   mit

65

dir;   manch   bun — — — te   Blu — — men   sind

68

an   dem   Strand;   mei - ne   Mut — ter   hat__ manch'

Anthology 38   Continued

71 gül - - - den Ge - wand". Mein Va - ter, mein Va - ter, und hö - rest du

76 nicht, was Er - len - kö - nig mir lei - se ver - spricht? Sei

81 ru - hig, blei - be ru - hig, mein Kind; in dür - ren Blät - tern säu - selt der Wind.

86 "Willst, fei - ner— Kna - be, du mit mir gehn? mei - ne Töch - ter sol - len dich

♪♪ Anthology 38   Continued

90
war - ten schön; mei - ne Töch - ter___ füh - ren den nächt - li - chen Reihn, und

93
wie - gen und tan - zen und sin - gen dich ein, sie wie - gen und tan - zen und

96
sin - gen dich ein." Mein Va - ter, mein Va - ter, und siehst du nicht

101
dort Erl - kö - nigs Töch - ter am dü - stern Ort? Mein Sohn, mein

Anthology 38   Continued

Anthology 38   Continued

127

an!   Erl - kö - nig hat mir ein Leids ge - than!

132   *accelerando*

Dem Va - - ter grau - set's, er rei - tet gesch -

cresc.

136

wind,   er hält in Ar - men das äch - zen - de

140

Kind,   er - reicht den Hof mit Müh und

Anthology 38   Continued

Who rides so late through night and wind?
It is a father with his child;
He holds the boy in his arm,
He clasps him tight, he keeps him warm.

"My son, why hidest thy face in fear?"
"Seest thou not, Father, the Erlking?
The Erlking with crown and train?"
"My son, 'tis but a streak of mist."

"O dear child, come away with me!
Lovely games I'll play with thee!
Many-colored flowers grow by the shore,
My mother has many golden robes."

"My father, my father, hearest thou not
What Erlking softly promises me?"
"Be calm, be calm, my child;"

"Fair boy, wilt thou come with me?
My lovely daughters shall wait on thee;
My daughters keep their nightly revels;
They will rock thee, dance, and sing thee to sleep."

"My father, my father, seest thou not
Erlking's daughers in that dark place?"
"My son, my son, I see clearly;
It is only the gleam of the old gray willows."

"I love thee, thy fair form ravishes me;
And if thou art not willing, I'll take thee by force."
"My father, my father, now he is seizing me!
Erlking has done me harm!"

The father shudders, he rides fast,
And holds in his arm the moaning child;
He reaches home with effort and toil:
In his arms the child lay dead!

Anthology 39   **Franz Schubert** (1797–1828), Waltz op. 9, no. 14

Anthology 41   **Franz Schubert** (1797–1828), Ecossaise no. 2, from *Waltzer, Ländler und Ecossaisen*, op. 18

Anthology 42   **Franz Schubert** (1797–1828), "Auf dem Flusse," from *Die Winterreise*

1 Langsam.

Der du so lu-stig rausch-test, du

hel-ler, wil-der Fluss, wie still bist du ge-wor-den, giebst kei-nen Schei-de gruss!

Mit har-ter, star-rer Rin-de hast du dich ü-ber-deckt, liegst kalt und un-be-weg-lich im

San-de aus-ge-streckt.   In   dei-ne De-cke grab' ich mit

Anthology 42 Continued

Anthology 42   Continued

Anthology 42   Continued

schwillt,   ob's wohl auch so— rei - ssend schwillt, ob's wohl

auch so— rei - ssend schwillt?

On the Stream

You that were once so merry,
You leaping laughing burn,
Are fallen into silence,
No greeting you return.

With crust all hard and frozen
You now are overspread.
You lie there cold and moveless
Upon your sandy bed.

I'll take a sharp-edged pebble,
And on your surface white
The name of my beloved
With hour and day I'll write.

The day of our first greeting,
The day when last we met.
And round the name and fingers
A broken ring I'll set.

My heart, within this
brooklet
Do you your image know?
Beneath its frozen surface
How turbulent its flow!
Ah, how turbulent its flow!

Anthology 43   **Fanny Mendelssohn Hensel** (1805–1847), "Bitte," from *Six Songs*, op. 7

Gaze on me for a while you dark eye, bring your full power into play, earnest, gentle, dreamy, unfathomable sweet night.
Take with your magic darkness this world away from me, that over my life you alone shall hover for ever and for ever.

Anthology 44   **Frédéric Chopin** (1810–1849), Mazurka 43 in Gm, op. posth. 67, no. 2

Anthology 44   Continued

Anthology 45   **Frédéric Chopin** (1810–1849), Mazurka 49 in Fm, op. posth. 68, no. 4

Anthology 46   **Robert Schumann** (1810–1856), Kinder Sonate no. 1, from *Three Piano Sonatas for the Young*, op. 118a

Anthology 46 Continued

Anthology 47   **Robert Schumann** (1810–1856), "Ich grolle nicht," from *Dichterliebe,* op. 48, mm. 1–19

I hold no resentment,
And even if my heart breaks,
O love forever lost,
I hold no resentment.
And although you gleam in jewelled splendor,
There falls no ray upon your heart's night,
I've long known it.

Anthology 48   **Robert Schumann** (1810–1856), "Widmung," from *Myrthen*, op. 25

Innig, lebhaft.

Du mei-ne See - le, du mein Herz, du mei-ne

Wonn', o du mein Schmerz, du mei-ne Welt, in der ich le - be, mein Him - mel

du, dar - ein ich schwe - be, o du mein Grab, in das hin -

Anthology 48   Continued

♪ Anthology 48   Continued

You, my soul, you my heart,
You, my delight, you, my grief,
You, my world, in which I live,
You my heaven, into which I soar,
O you my grave, in which forever
I have laid my sorrow!
You are the rest, you are the peace,
You are sent from heaven to me.
That you love me makes me worthy,
Your glance has transfigured me,
Your love lifts me above myself,
My good spirit, my better self!

You, my soul, you my heart,
You, my delight, you, my grief,
You, my world, in which I live,
You my heaven, into which I soar,
My good spirit, my better self!

Anthology 49   **Robert Schumann** (1810–1856), "Am leuchtenden Sommermorgen," from *Dichterliebe*, op. 48

Anthology 49   **Continued**

stumm.   Es flü - stern und spre - chen die Blu - men,   und

schau'n mit - lei - dig mich an;   *pp Langsamer.* Sei uns - er Schwe - ster nicht bö - se,   du

ritard. trau - ri - ger, blas - - ser Mann.

Anthology 49   Continued

"On a bright summer morning"

On a bright summer morning
I walk around the garden.
The flowers are whispering and speaking,
But I walk in silence.

The flowers are whispering and speaking,
and they look with pity on me;
Be not angry with our sister,
You sorrowful, pale man.

Im klagenden Ton

Anthology 51   **Franz Liszt** (1811–1886), *Consolation* no. 4

Anthology 52   **Giuseppe Verdi** (1813–1901), "Libiamo ne'lieti calici," from *La traviata,* mm. 22–42

Let's drink of the joyful goblets
That beauty adorns with flowers
And the fleeting hour will get drunk
With sensual pleasure

Anthology 53   **Giuseppe Verdi** (1813–1901), *Il trovatore*, act II, no. 11, mm. 1–11

Azucena: plunge this blade up to the hilt into the heart of the cruel one.
        Strike!
Manrico: Yes, I swear it. This blade will descend into the heart of the cruel one.

Anthology 54   **Giuseppe Verdi** (1813–1901), *Il trovatore*, act II, no. 14, mm. 15–24

Me! I turn to Him
Who alone can dry the mourner's tears
of sorrow, and when my days of
grief are over, mercy eternal may
guide my weary spirit
yet to meet him again.

Anthology 55   **Giuseppe Verdi** (1813–1901), "Celeste Aida," from *Aida*, mm. 1–29

Anthology 55   Continued

18
cin - to___   dir - ti: per te ho pu - gna - to,   per te ho vin - to!
splen - dor,   say - ing: For you I con - quered.   See your de - fend - er!

f   *ff*

22

pp

Andantino. (♩ = 116)

27   *con espress.*
Ce - le - ste A - i - da,___
Fair - est___ A - i - da,___

p   *m.s.*

℗ed.

Früh, wann die Häh - ne krähn eh' die Stern - lein

schwind - en muss ich am Her - de stehn, muss Feu - er zün - den.

Schön ist der Flam - men Schein, es spring - en die Fun - ken: Ich schaue so da - rein,

etwas lebhafter

in Leid ver - sun - ken

Plötz - lich,   da

etwas ruhiger

kommt es mir,   treu - lo - ser Kna be,   dass ich die Nacht von dir ge -

wie zu Anfang

träu - met ha - be.

Trä - ne auf

Trä - ne dann stür - zet her - nie - der; so kommt der Tag her - an   o ging' er

wie - der!

Early, when the cocks crow,
Before the stars fade out,
I must stand at the hearth
And light the fire.

Lovely is the flames' light
With its flying sparks;
I gaze into it,
Deep in sorrow.

Suddenly I remember,
Faithless boy,
That I in the night
Of thee have dreamed.

Tear on tear
Tumbles down;
So begins the day—
O, would it were ended!

Anthology 58   **Richard Strauss** (1864–1949), "Ruhe, meine Seele!," op. 27, no. 1

Anthology 59   **Amy Beach** (1867–1944), *Ecstasy*

dear - est,   have   we not to-geth - er   One long,   bright

day_____   of love, so   glad   and free?

On - ly to

♪♪ Anthology 59   Continued

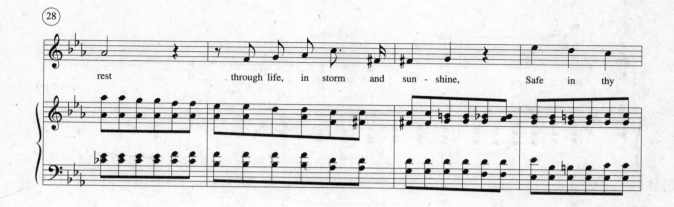

28

rest   through life, in storm and sun - shine,   Safe in thy

32

breast,   where sor - row   dare   not   fly;   Ah dear - - est,

cresc.   *f*   *f*

𝄋𝄢 Ped.   *

36

dear - est,   thus   in sweet - est rap - ture   With thee to

Ped.   *   Ped.   *   Ped.   *

live, _____ with thee at last ____ to die! _____